MW01251676

Journey to Divine Purpose

Discover Keys to Living an Extraordinary
Life of Faith and
Fulfilling Your Divine Purpose

Mary Elizabeth Foster

Cover design by SM Designs
Flushing, Michigan USA

ISBN: 978-1539046110

Acknowledgments

I extend the highest gratitude to God for giving me the vision to complete this written work. Initially, I was skeptical of writing as there were several demands being placed on my time. My role as a wife, mother, and career woman can be time-consuming. But, God imparted grace and anointed me to complete this work. To God be the Glory!

I thank my husband for his unwavering support and encouragement. Through our quiet times of prayer, he encouraged me to write the vision for others in the body of Christ. Special thanks to my mother for being a "tiger mom" and pushing me to excel in all aspects of life. I love you mom! I thank my sister who has been a great blessing in my life. I thank my three beautiful children: Anna Danielle, Benjamin Micah and Eden Elizabeth who remained silent during critical times of writing and allowed their mother to complete this divine assignment. Lastly, I thank my pastor and his wife for their encouragement and support of my ministry.

TABLE OF CONTENTS

Foreword

Mary Elizabeth Foster is a devoted wife, mother, and committed worshipper of our Lord and Savior Jesus Christ. Since coming to faith in Christ, she has demonstrated an unfailing love for the Savior.

In this period of Post Modernism, Mary's Christ-centered relationship has served as a light in darkness and she has uniquely modeled biblical womanhood to a generation that lacks moral absolutes, biblical submission, and biblical knowledge. Her zeal and thirst for the Word of God is evident throughout the pages of this written work, *Journey to Divine Purpose*. Each Chapter is designed to deepen and develop the believer's walk through the sanctifying work of the Holy Spirit, while disciplining and preparing the reader to walk in their divine call and destiny. No doubt this book represents the clear purpose and pathway that God has carved out for Mary Foster. Surely, her life of prayer, worship, and inductive study has qualified her to express God's truths in written form.

This is a book that can be read in one sitting, as well as one that will serve as a tool that can be referred to throughout the corridor of time, to edify, encourage, and equip the reader through the power of God's Word. I believe this book will be a special blessing to you.

Evangelist Christina Lee
Nehemiah Training & Consulting
Charlotte, North Carolina

Introduction

Our divine purpose is ordained and established in heaven before we are born or become citizens of planet earth. Then, it is revealed or made known in the earth. This is proven when God reveals this truth to the prophet Jeremiah. God says, *"Before I formed thee in the belly I knew thee; and before thou camest forth out of the womb I sanctified thee, and I ordained thee a prophet unto the nations"* (Jeremiah 1:5). Before Jeremiah's birth, his calling to be a prophet was ordained. Jeremiah questioned his ability to operate as a prophet to the nation of Israel, citing his youthfulness and inexperienced oratorical skills to God. Jeremiah made the mistake, as some occasionally do, of assuming that he was not qualified for the position or prepared to take on the divine challenge. But, when the all-knowing, all-powerful God selects you for a position or an assignment, he has full confidence that you can accomplish the task by his empowering grace. God tells Jeremiah, *"Say not, I am a child: for thou shalt go to all that I shall send thee, and whatsoever I command thee, thou shalt speak"* (Jeremiah 1:7). As in the case of Jeremiah, God desires that we fulfill the divine purpose he has established for our lives. He does not want us to depart planet earth with the legacy of living an unfulfilled life. The responsibility of fulfilling our divine purpose is placed on us.

Journey to Divine Purpose serves as a blueprint for living an extraordinary life of faith in Christ and fulfilling your divine purpose. You will gain a deeper understanding of foundational Christian principles that help to nurture and develop your faith.

Each chapter is designed to help you experience the truth of God's Word, serve as a source of encouragement and spark your interest in developing a consistent life of devotion to God. You will draw practical solutions to life challenges and be introduced to kingdom principles to follow in your daily Christian living. You will be stimulated to look into the Bible and glean truths from the experiences of various biblical characters some of which made extraordinary sacrifices and fulfilled their divine purpose.

My prayer is that you will have an encounter with the living God as you read this book. My earnest desire is that your passion to pursue and fulfill your divine purpose will be far greater after reading this book than previous. Allocate time to allow the Holy Spirit to minister to your heart as you read each chapter. I believe you will be inspired to deepen your walk with God, increase your level of faith, and fulfill your divine purpose. May God bless you abundantly as you read.

Chapter One

Destiny-Altering Decisions

The steps of a good man [woman] are ordered by the Lord: and he delighteth in his way.

Psalms 37:23

Destiny altering decisions involve the act of changing one's life or circumstances in a substantial way so that their life is in alignment with the will of God. Destiny altering decisions are interwoven into the Christian experience. These decisions are inescapable and unavoidable. You will encounter the opportunity to make such decisions as you continue to grow in faith. Those who ignore the reality of making destiny altering decisions end up living an unfulfilled life. Unfortunately, these individuals become stationary as they are unable to manage the responsibility that comes with making such a decision. Jesus requires that His followers diligently seek Him in order to receive counsel, wisdom, and instruction for life direction. Jesus says, *"But, seek ye first the kingdom of God, and His righteousness; and all these things shall be added unto you"* (St. Matthew 6:33). Seeking the kingdom of God must be a number one life priority. This includes maintaining a committed life of prayer and sincere devotion to God through the study of his word. When seeking the kingdom of God is the number one life priority, the promises that follow are richly rewarding. God honors your diligence and persistence. Unlike those who place other life priorities over the kingdom of God, you experience the divine blessing of having a fulfilled life here on earth.

There are countless examples in scripture of people who made destiny altering decisions and fulfilled their divine purpose. These individuals left their past life and accepted a brand new life in God. For most, this meant severing social connections, familial ties and relationships. When examining destiny altering decisions, two biblical characters who come to mind are the Old Testament patriarchs of faith Sarah and her husband Abraham. Their walk of faith began with making a destiny altering decision. We will examine the life of Sarah and

Abraham and highlight lessons we can learn from their experience with making such a decision.

Humble Beginnings

Abraham is introduced in scripture by the name "Abram" which means *exalted father*. His name was changed by God to "Abraham" which means *father of many* (see Genesis 17:5). Sarah is introduced in scripture by the name "Sarai". The name "Sarai" is derived from the Hebrew word *sar* which means a head person of any rank or class, princess, ruler or steward. [1] The name "Sarah" is a primitive root of the word "Sarai" meaning to prevail or have power as a *princess*.[2] Sarai's name was changed to Sarah by God (see Genesis 17:15). The God given name Sarah would be used throughout time to denote her godly character and unwavering faith in God's promise to her husband Abraham.

Scripture notes that Sarah was barren or unable to have children (see Genesis 11:30). She was far beyond childbearing years when scripture begins the account of her life. Due to her advanced years of age, there was no hope of ever becoming pregnant and providing descendants to her husband. During biblical times, womanhood was defined by one's ability to reproduce children. Women who bore children were held in

---

[1] James Strong, LL.D., S.T.D., *The New Strong's Exhaustive Concordance of the Bible*, (Nashville, Tennessee: Thomas Nelson Publishers, 1995 – 96).

[2] ibid.

high regard and received respect in their community as opposed to women who were unable to bear children. In the case of Sarah, it would take God's miraculous intervention to bring about a biological child for her and Abraham to enjoy.

Destiny Altering Decisions Require Assuming a
Heavenly Identity

Destiny altering decisions require that you assume a heavenly identity. Sarah and her husband identified as strangers and pilgrims on the earth (see Hebrews 11:13). The terms "stranger" and "pilgrim" denote a lack of permanency in a foreign region. In the case of Sarah and Abraham, this meant both recognized that they were not permanent dwellers of this world. The world was not their eternal home. They did not consider the regions they traveled and settled for a period of time as their permanent dwelling place. They were citizens of heaven and after God spoke to Abraham regarding the promises, the course of their lives changed and became heavenly centered. As heavenly citizens, Sarah and Abraham made a decision to alienate themselves from the desires of the temporal life that surrounded them and adopt a life centered on pleasing God. Their identity as heavenly citizens enabled them to trust God and patiently wait for the manifestation of God's promises. If they valued living in Haran more than God's directive to leave that city, they would have stumbled along the way and not completed their journey of faith. Hebrews 11:15 says, *"And truly, if they had been mindful of that country from whence they came out, they might have opportunity to have returned."* There was no turning back to Haran once their journey began.

Sarah and Abraham did not leave Haran alone. Their nephew Lot and his wife journeyed with them (see Genesis 12:4). Lot accompanied them until Abraham advised that he, his family and herdsman settle in another region. Both had herds, tents, and flocks but the land could not support them while living together. Plus, the herdsman of Lot was at constant odds with Abraham's herdsman, creating a quarrelsome environment. I suppose this may have created some tension in their uncle-nephew relationship. Lot saw that the plain of Jordan was well watered and he settled in that region. Genesis 13:10,11 says, *"And Lot lifted up his eyes, and beheld all the plain of Jordan, that it was well watered everywhere, before the Lord destroyed Sodom and Gomorrah, even as the garden of the Lord, like the land of Egypt, as thou comest unto Zoar. Then, Lot chose him all the plain of Jordan; and Lot journeyed east: and they separated themselves the one from the other."* While the cities looked appealing from a distance and appeared to be a desirable region to live, they were the epitome of sin. *"But the men of Sodom were wicked and sinners before the Lord exceedingly"* (Genesis 13:13). We do not see evidence in scripture of Lot consulting the Lord or seeking godly counsel to find the region God purposed for him, his family and staff of herdsman to settle. Lot makes his decision strictly based on appearance. What a big mistake! It is important to consult the Lord in our decision making and not develop a habit of making decisions strictly based on appearance or what is being presented. We should make decisions that keep us in the will of God and not draw us away from God's intended purposes.

Assuming a heavenly identity plays an important role in the fulfillment of our divine purpose. When we come to faith in Christ, we are to center our focus on that which is of eternal value or significance. Our affection is to be heavenly. Our life is in Christ who is the giver and sustainer of our faith. Colossians 3: 1 – 3 says, *"If ye then be risen with Christ, seek those things which are above, where Christ sitteth on the right hand of God. Set your affection on things above, not on things on the earth. For ye are dead, and your life is hid with Christ in God."* If our affection is earthly, we will live a temporal centered life and our salvation witness will have little to no impact. On the other hand, if our affection is heavenly, we are in a position to have greater impact on the expansion of God's kingdom, and see God intervene and bless our lives as well as the lives of those we are to influence.

Early in my walk of faith, the Holy Spirit revealed to me the importance of Colossians 3: 1 - 3. Just as I was waking up for the day, the Holy Spirit spoke the following words to my heart, "set your affection on things above". I referenced Colossians Chapter Three and meditated on the first three verses. At the time, I had several concerns as a graduate student: finances, funding for my last semester of school, finding employment, paying bills, and a few other cares. As I meditated, I began to see the importance of assuming my heavenly identity. I saw the need to live by faith and give my cares to Jesus. I made a commitment to center my life on pleasing God and be obedient to his word. Within a year, I successfully completed graduate school and obtained a permanent full-time job in my desired career field. All my needs were met. I rejoiced of how God intervened and blessed my life greatly.

Destiny Altering Decisions May Require Departure

Destiny altering decisions may require departure from familiar surroundings in order to accomplish God's greater purposes. Sarah's journey of faith begins with her and Abraham leaving the land of Haran to travel to the land of Canaan. God's command to her husband Abraham was: *"Get thee out of thy country, and from thy kindred, and from thy father's house, unto a land that I will shew thee"* (Genesis 12:1). The command God had given to Abraham served as a life changing directive for Abraham and Sarah. God was instructing both to abandon their pagan roots and follow his plan of faith. Sarah and Abraham leaving Haran was a destiny altering decision that changed the entire course of their lives. At the time both departed, they did not recognize the substantial impact the decision to leave their familiar place of residency would have on their family and future generations who would come to faith in Jesus Christ. Let's examine each aspect of God's command to leave Haran closely.

Departure from Country

God required departure from their country, the geographical region where both resided. Country is figurative of the place of familiarity and comfort. You can become content with your surroundings, and not envision the need to change, move forward or progress beyond it. The plan of God will require that you depart from the place of familiarity and comfort and trust God for further life direction. According to historical record, Haran is present day Iraq. During the time of Sarah, Haran was a prosperous center of religion and industry. It was a center of early civilization. Thousands of recovered

15

clay documents attest to thriving business activity. Excavations of the royal cemetery have revealed a surprisingly advanced culture, particularly in the arts and crafts. Uncovered were beautiful jewelry and art treasures, including headwear, personal jewelry, and exquisite china and crystal. [3] Haran was one of the most desirable cities to live during Sarah's time. Sarah and her husband Abraham were prosperous there. They had servants, handmaidens, herdsman, and owned land. But, in spite of all the wealth and material possessions both accumulated, they were not living in the will of God. Both desperately needed God's divine intervention in their lives. Prosperity and the volume of material resources are not indicators of being in alignment with God's will. We are to rely on the leading and direction of the Holy Spirit and not the amount of wealth or material possessions we have to determine if we are in the will of the Lord or operating within his divine plan.

Departure from Kindred

God commanded that Sarah and her husband separate from their kindred. This directive included separation from their family connections and close-knit ties. Haran was known to be a pagan worshipping society. The residents worshipped false gods. The worship of false gods was a part of their kindred's customs and practices. In order for Sarah and Abraham to inherit the blessings of God, both had to leave their family connections in Haran and establish a family legacy of faith. For Sarah and Abraham, following God's command

[3] Herbert Lockyer, Sr. with F.F. Bruce and R.K. Harrison, *Illustrated Dictionary of the Bible*, (Nashville, Tennessee: Thomas Nelson Publishers, 1986).

would require departing from the influence of paganism to receive a greater promise from the one and true living God.

Departure from Father's House

Sarah and Abraham became citizens of Haran as a result of traveling with their father Terah who left his country of origin to journey to the land of Canaan but did not continue with the journey. Instead, he chose to become a resident of Haran. The family settled in Haran and adopted the idolatrous customs common to that region. Joshua 24:2 says, *"... Your fathers dwelt on the other side of the flood in old time, even Terah, the father of Abraham, and the father of Nachor: and they served other gods."* Terah was an idolater. He did not worship the one and true living God. He was not a man of godly faith. God's plan included Sarah and her husband completing Terah's journey and their lives serving as a well-spring of blessings to future generations.

God's Divine Directive Requires Obedience

Obedience is adherence to God's instruction, directive or command. A God given directive or command requires submission to the authority of God and allowing Him to be in supreme control over your life direction and purpose. As demonstrated in the life of Sarah and her husband, God will fulfill His promise when we commit to obey His directive. When God instructed Abraham to leave Haran, he and Sarah did not contemplate if they heard from the Lord correctly. They obeyed the voice of the Lord and departed. Their familiar country was the place where they were comfortable living. At the time of their departure, they did not have all the details from God but were confident that God would be with them. *"By faith Abraham, when he was called to go out into a place which he should after receive for an inheritance, obeyed; and he went out, not knowing whither he went"* (Hebrews 11:8).

If I were Sarah, perhaps I would have pondered a few questions such as how do I say goodbye to longtime friends and acquaintances, or how do I part company with family members and establish new relationships. Perhaps, Sarah pondered such questions but the important point to consider is that she took a leap of faith by following her husband and trusted God to reveal the remaining portion of His plan for their lives. She accepted the directive God gave to Abraham as her divine directive and did not seek a life independent of God. The act of voluntarily submitting our will to God is mandatory. If we do not voluntarily surrender our will to God, we will not fulfill God's divine purpose for our lives. The Bible tells us, *"If ye be willing and obedient, ye shall eat the good of the land"* (Isaiah 1:19). Notice that willingness and obedience are connected in this scripture passage. Obedience must be accompanied by a willing heart. Sarah and her husband's obedience to God's command confirmed their willingness to surrender personal desires and plans to accomplish God's will. As exampled by Sarah and Abraham, when we willingly surrender our personal desires and plans to God, God intervenes in the course of our lives to bring about his best for us.

Now, let's compare the land of Haran with the land of promise to get an understanding of the blessings imparted to Sarah and her husband for adhering to God's divine directive.

The Land of Haran

- Life of Social Comfort
- Riches and prosperity limited to Haran
- Unfulfilled Life
- Barren, Unable to Reproduce
- No Kingdom Inheritance
- Unknown to future generations
- Legacy limited to one or a few generations

The Land of Promise

- Life of Faith
- Riches and prosperity unlimited & provided to future generations
- Fulfilled Life
- Fruitful, Child Bearer
- Kingdom of God Inheritance
- Known as 'Father' to future generations
- Known as 'Princess' to future generations
- A lasting legacy of faith

Sarah was living in a desirable region, had strong familial ties, and a great amount of material possessions. She was living a comfortable life in the land of Haran. But, her life as she was accustomed to living changed following her adherence to the spoken directive God issued to her husband Abraham. Hebrews 11:9 notes that they wandered in tents and temporary dwelling places after leaving Haran. Both endured the reality of not having a place of permanency in fulfillment of God's promise for their lives. Scripture does not provide us with Sarah's initial reaction to Abraham's call to leave their pagan centered dwelling place. But, we do know that she willingly journeyed with him. Additionally, the details were not made clear by God to Sarah or Abraham at the time the directive to leave was given but God provided a promise that included divine blessings if both were obedient. *"And I will make of thee a great nation, and I will bless thee, and make thy name great; and thou shalt be a blessing: And I will bless them that bless thee, and curse him that curseth thee: and in thee shall all families of the earth be blessed"* (Genesis 12:2, 3). Obedience to a God given directive is always accompanied by a promise. In the case of Sarah and Abraham, God made several promises.

God's Promises

- He will make him a great nation and bless him (Genesis 12:2a)
- He will make his name great and he would serve as a blessing (Genesis 12:2b)
- He will bless those who bless him and curse those who curse him (Genesis 12:3)
- All families of the earth will be blessed through him (Genesis 12:3b)
- He will be a father of many nations and greatly fruitful (Genesis 17:5, 6)
- A child who will be his heir (Genesis 15:4)
- Descendants as numerous as the stars of the sky (Genesis 15:5)
- Promised land for his descendants (Genesis 15:18 – 21; Genesis 17:8)

God also promised Abraham that Sarah would be blessed of the Lord. She would give birth to a son and kings of people will be of her lineage. She would be known as a mother of nations. God promised Sarah an honor that would follow her throughout the ages of time. God revealed these promises to Abraham at a time in which his life situation dictated otherwise. For example, Abraham was promised descendants but Isaac was not yet born. Sarah's promise included giving birth to a son but she was far beyond childbearing years. God will sometimes reveal his promises to us at a time when our life situation seems far removed from the manifestation. This should prompt us to increase our level of faith, trust God and follow his prescribed plan. When we do, we are rewarded. Has God spoken a promise to you? Remember, when God declares a promise, he declares it from the vantage point of eternity. He is counting on you to put your faith into action to fulfill his promise. *"In the same way, faith by itself, if it is not accompanied by action, is dead"* (James 2:17, NIV). Have you made a written note of God's promise to you? If you haven't already, make a written note. God is truthful and will fulfill his promise. *"God is not a man, that he should lie, nor a son of man, that he should change his mind. Does he speak and then not act? Does he promise and not fulfill"* (Numbers 23:19, NIV).

Destiny Altering Decisions Require Patience with God's Timing

I think one of the most noted shortcomings unveiled in the life of Sarah was her lack of patience with God's timing. Sarah was not totally convinced that she would be the one to birth the promise child. Therefore, she derived a plan to give her maidservant Hagar to Abraham for the purpose of bearing a child. During Sarah's time period, it was not uncommon for wives who were barren to give their maidservants to their husbands for the purpose of bearing children. In some cases, maidservants served as surrogate mothers for barren wives. But, Sarah's plan of giving Hagar to Abraham was of her own doing. This plan was not initiated, inspired or motivated by God. God's plan did not involve a maidservant giving birth to the child. God is a God of divine order. He does not decree a command and then violate the principles of his word. When God spoke to Abraham and said that the child would come from his loins, Sarah was his wife and God was speaking in terms of Sarah being the one to deliver the child of promise. God would have never allowed another woman to enter into their marital relationship to give birth to the promise child. Doing such would have been contrary to his word and nature. Know that when God gives a promise to your spouse, you are included in the promise. You must see yourself as being a part of God's promise to your spouse. If your spouse is in ministry and God has spoken a promise concerning the growth and success of the ministry your spouse leads, you play a key and instrumental role in birthing that promise into being. You are not a sideline spectator. You help to birth God's promise into existence.

Sarah, in haste of God's divine manifestation of the promise child, gave Hagar to Abraham, and a child was conceived (see Genesis 16: 1 – 4). After Hagar became pregnant, she began to despise Sarah. Sarah, in turn began to mistreat Hagar and Hagar fled for a period of time. While on the run, Hagar was confronted by an angel of the Lord who instructed her to return to Sarah's house. Hagar listened to the instructions of the angel and returned to Sarah and Abraham's home giving birth to a son who Abraham named Ishmael. In God's timing, Sarah would later give birth to the child of promise Isaac. Isaac's birth occurred when Sarah was well advanced in age and it served as the fulfillment of God's promise to her and Abraham. What we learn from the life mistake of Sarah is that when we move outside of God's appointed timing; we do not accelerate the manifestation of God's promise. Instead, actions initiated by impatience only put into motion consequences that were not intended. Then, we are subject to live with the consequences that follow actions motivated by impatience with God's plan.

Galatians 5: 23 – 26 provides an allegorical illustration of what each son born to Abraham represented. The son born to Hagar represents those who continue to live in bondage to the legalities and unattainable requirements of the old covenant. They live by the notion that they must labor and toil to obtain their righteousness. They believe that they must do this or that to receive righteousness. This belief is outside of God's plan of righteousness. Sarah represents those who live under the blessing of the new covenant and received righteousness by faith in Christ. When we come to faith in Christ, we are made righteous in the sight of God. Righteousness is credited to us as a result of our faith. Just as Isaac, we are the children of promise. And, as children of promise, we are entitled to all of God's promises and blessings.

Destiny Altering Decisions Can Lead to the Establishment of a Legacy of Faith

Sarah and Abraham's destiny altering decision led to the establishment of a legacy of faith that served as a blessing to their family and multiple generations to follow. They are honored as the mother and father of all who live by faith in Christ because of their faithfulness to God's promise. They endured, though at the time they answered the call to leave Haran, they did not know what to expect. Throughout their journey of faith, the understanding of God's promise grew and they became thoroughly convinced that God would manifest what was promised. Sarah and Abraham made mistakes along their journey but they did not stop. They did not quit. They did not give up. Both learned the value of believing God and completely relying on his truth. Their faith experience shows that when you make a commitment to believe God, you align yourself to receive heaven's best. And, when God unveils His plan for our lives, it is his desire to establish a legacy of faith that extends to multiple generations. Others will be impacted and blessed by our life of faith.

The life of Jonathan Edwards, an American revivalist preacher from the 1700s, serves as a perfect example of establishing and leaving a legacy of faith that extends to multiple generations. Jonathan Edwards' most famously noted sermon *Sinners in the Hand of an Angry God* is still being circulated, studied and impacting the lives of people today. Jonathan Edwards and his wife devoted themselves to creating a family of faith. History tells us that they focused on rearing godly children. At the turn of the twentieth century, educator and pastor A.E. Winship traced the family lineage of Jonathan Edwards one-hundred and fifty years following his earthly demise. The results of Winship's study were astounding. There were stark differences between the lineage of Jonathan Edwards and a man named Max Jukes. From the lineage of Jonathan Edwards was a United States Vice President, United States Senators, judges, professors, public office holders, lawyers, preachers and missionaries. Edwards' descendants were healthy and long-lived. Prosperity and success followed the descendants of Jonathan Edwards. On the other hand, the family tree of Max Jukes was traced to forty-two different men in the New York prison system. From the family lineage of Max Jukes were murderers, thieves, womanizers and paupers. Unfortunately, Jukes' legacy served as a great liability to the state. But, the life and legacy of Jonathan Edwards served as a benefit to future generations. It is without question that a legacy of faith serves as a great asset to you, your family and multiple generations that come from your family tree.

When examining the establishment of a legacy of faith, I also think of our nation. Our nation was birthed by pilgrims seeking religious freedom. These pilgrims separated from the Church of England and left their homeland in search of a new place to settle. The decision to leave England was destiny altering. They desired to live in a land where they could worship God in spirit and in truth. They would settle in a new land that became their home. Their journey to America later led to the formation of a government established on biblical principles. Many American missionaries and revivalists have impacted and blessed the world by traveling globally to pioneer churches, build Christian based schools and spread the gospel. Much of this would not be possible, had it not been for those who in faith journeyed to America. Though America seems far from its Christian heritage, if the people of God pray in faith for a return to the heart of God, I believe we will see change. 2 Chronicles 7:14 says, *"If my people, which are called by my name, shall humble themselves, and pray, and seek my face, and turn from their wicked ways; then will I hear from heaven, and will forgive their sin, and will heal their land."*

My Destiny Altering Decision

Following the completion of undergraduate school, I began working full-time with a federal government agency. The government position was short-lived as the agency was closing operations within a few months. I committed to take a one-year break from pursuing educational goals to focus on obtaining employment outside the federal government and applying for graduate school. Much to my surprise, I was met with stiff competition in my job search. During the time, the job market in the Oakland-San Francisco Bay Area was highly competitive. I received several job interviews and noticed the highlighted mark surrounding the name of the undergraduate institution I attended. Yet, I did not receive follow-up phone calls or invitations for a second interview. The highlighted mark on my resume let me know that employers recognized the prestige that accompanied the undergraduate institution I attended but were not interested in hiring me to do the job.

During this one year break and following the closing of operations with the federal agency, I obtained a position as a substitute schoolteacher and took advantage of the consultation service my undergraduate institution offered to recent graduates. The consultation service included me meeting on a consistent basis with a career advisor who coached me along the graduate school application process. As I began gathering application materials for graduate schools, a divine knowing to apply to graduate schools in the Midwest entered my heart. This divine knowing was distinct in that I had an immediate understanding that the Midwest should be the place of my residency for graduate school. Understand that I was born and raised in the state of California, a state of plentiful sunshine and beauty. The notion of residency in the Midwest would not have been a thought I would've considered independently. I would have contemplated the unwelcoming weather pattern the Midwest offers including bitter cold winters, humid summer months, rainy spring seasons, low temperature autumn months and periodic rain and thunderstorms. Most of which I was not accustomed as a California native. I was pleasantly content living in California and experiencing mild temperatures. Although the job market in California was highly competitive and the cost of living steadily rising, California would be the most ideal state for me to remain. But, I just as Sarah and Abraham had to make a destiny altering decision. My decision involved changing my residency by moving from California to the Midwest for the purpose of attending graduate school. And, much to my utter amazement, God's plan for my life extended beyond graduate school.

A few months following the submission of my graduate school application materials, I was notified by the University of Chicago that my name would be placed on a waiting list, with the possibility of delayed admittance or the opportunity to consider enrollment the following academic school year. Shortly after receiving correspondence from the University of Chicago, I got a phone call from the University of Michigan at

Ann Arbor notifying me of my acceptance into the Social Work graduate program. I was excited at the time the news was relayed by the university representative. I calmly accepted the offer to attend the University of Michigan and began the paperwork process to seal my acceptance. Just before the fall semester began, I departed from the place of the familiar, leaving family and long established friendships to land in the region of the Midwest. I did not know that at the time I acted on God's divine leading, I was journeying to the place of God's divine plan. His plan involved me meeting a young man at the University of Michigan who later became my husband, coming to sincere devotion and commitment to Christ, and establishing a Christ-centered family. God in His divine wisdom had other plans for my life that were far more detailed than I would have imagined or considered. I am glad that I followed God and yielded to the divine knowing to establish residency in the Midwest. If I had not made this destiny altering decision, I would not be accomplishing the purposes of God today.

In your salvation experience, you will make destiny altering decisions. You may be at the point of making a destiny altering decision right now. Destiny altering decisions such as accepting the call to ministry, pioneering a ministry effort, or uniting with a body of believers for Christian fellowship can be life changing. Everyday life examples of destiny altering decisions may include establishing a career after the completion of college, re-careering after job loss or retirement, entrepreneurship and as exampled in my life as well as the lives of Sarah and Abraham, geographical relocation. In our decision making, it is always best to consult God so that we act in accordance with his divine timetable. God gets the glory out of our lives when we make decisions that are in alignment with his purposes.

Key Principles

1. Destiny altering decisions are interwoven into the Christian experience. Expect to make destiny altering decisions.

2. Destiny altering decisions require releasing the past and embracing the future.

3. Destiny altering decisions require radical life changes.

4. Destiny altering decisions bring about a change in one's life perspective.

5. Destiny altering decisions impact the lives of present and future generations.

Prayer

Heavenly Father, the days of my life are pre-ordained by you and I accept your divine purpose for my life. I ask for your wisdom to make destiny altering decisions that are in alignment with your divine will. Let your Holy Spirit be my compass, as your Spirit is a safe guide. I declare that I will not be fearful or apprehensive about the next step to take in my journey of faith. Thank you for granting my request, in Jesus' name, Amen.

Study Questions for Chapter One are on pages 152 - 153

Chapter Two

Character Development

A good name is rather to be chosen than great riches, and loving favor rather than silver and gold.

Proverbs 22:1

The Importance of Character Development

Character development is necessary to be an effective witness of Jesus Christ. We live in a world surrounded by examples of unscrupulous behavior. People are determined to do whatever it takes to get ahead. Today, companies spend millions of dollars training employees on the importance of honesty and integrity, yet individuals embezzle funds, give false statements and indulge in reckless behavior that result in companies paying costly litigation settlements, all because of a lack of character. Believers must stand out as a beacon of light in our darkened world. In my reading of the scriptures, I've discovered that those who developed character earnestly pursued and received the promises of God in their generation. Their legacy of faith is one that can be emulated, followed and trusted. Those who failed in building character became terrors in biblical history. It is unfortunate that their lives serve as a reminder of what not to do.

The life of Saul, the first king of Israel, serves as an example of what not to do when elevated to a position of leadership. He failed to develop character. Scripture notes that Saul was head and shoulders above all others in Israel (see I Samuel 9:2). Saul was God's candidate of choice for king. Saul did not have to launch a campaign or seek the nomination of others for his position. He was divinely selected and appointed by God. (There is no greater blessing than to have the God of heaven select you for a position of leadership.) But, when you examine the life of Saul, it is evident that he valued his position as king more than his covenant relationship with God. He valued his kingship over submitting to the authority of our Lord. He failed to recognize the importance of submission to

God.   Instead, Saul valued catering to his own desires over pleasing God and fulfilling the purpose God intended for him as king over Israel.   Listed below is an outline of Saul's character and actions prior to and at the end of his kingship. Clearly, Saul digressed from the place of divine purpose.

Saul's Character & Actions Before and at the Start of Kingship

- Young and Impressive (I Samuel 9:2)
- Humble and Sincere (I Samuel 15:17)
- Obedient (I Samuel 9: 3,4)
- Chosen of God to lead Israel (I Samuel 9: 16,17; I Samuel 10:24)
- God was with Him (I Samuel 10:7)
- Heart changed by God (I Samuel 10:9)
- The Spirit of God fell on him in power and he joined the prophets in prophesying (I Samuel 10:10,11)
- Valued going to the place of God's presence (I Samuel 10:13)
- Peaceful spirit when he was despised by some who opposed his selection as king (I Samuel 10:27)

Saul's Character & Actions During and at the End of Kingship

- Disobedient (I Samuel 13: 13,14; I Samuel 15:19 - 22)
- Rebellious and Arrogant (I Samuel 15:23)
- Fearful (I Samuel 15:24)
- Rejected by God as king of Israel (I Samuel 16:1)
- The Spirit of God departed from him and he was tormented by an evil spirit (I Samuel 16:14)

- Heart filled with jealousy (I Samuel 18: 8,9)
- A Murderer (I Samuel 22: 17 – 19)

In Old Testament times, it was customary for kings who went to war to plunder their enemy's possessions, force them into slavery, capture their king, and take their livestock and material wealth.   During the reign of Saul, Israel went to war with the Amalekites. Saul was instructed by the prophet Samuel to kill all inhabitants, their livestock and king. Samuel said to Saul, *"Now go and smite Amalek, and utterly destroy all that they have, and spare them not; but slay both man and woman, infant and suckling, ox and sheep, camel and donkey"* (I Samuel 15:3).   God's instructions were very thorough. He made it clear that Saul was to destroy the Amalekites and all that they possessed. Saul, choosing to satisfy his own likings, did not adhere to God's instructions. Instead, he kept the King of Amalek alive and saved the best livestock for sacrifices. He used the livestock taken from their enemy in a sacrificial offering to the Lord. Saul was supposing that he could atone for his wrongdoing through sacrifices. But, this did not work with God. God is a holy God and he demands adherence to his instructions. Saul's act of disobedience was so detestable to God that He sent the prophet Samuel to relay his message of divine judgment.   Saul was rejected by God for his rebellious act against God's instructions and his kingship was taken away.   *"… The Lord hath rent the kingdom of Israel from thee this day, and hath given it to a neighbor of thine, that is better than thou"* (I Samuel 15:28). He spent the remainder of his kingship years holding the title of king but trying to take the life of David, the one God anointed to be his successor.   Unfortunately, Saul's life ended tragically on the battlefield and serves as a reminder of the necessity to develop character. We should value our covenant relationship with the

Lord first. If our focus becomes a position or ministry gifting and its benefits, we miss the blessing of knowing the Lord intimately. We can become acquainted with the politics of a position, the administrative demands, and accompanying tasks. Unintentionally, our focus can easily shift from committing actions that build character to actions that emulate poor character. How many times have you heard of a person who started out good, trustworthy and sincere and through time became corrupt? They simply lost focus and as in the case of Saul, lacked an earnest commitment to please God. For Saul, this ultimately resulted in the loss of his position as king and death. The life of the Old Testament Israelite Joseph serves as an example of one who developed character in spite of challenging and difficult circumstances.

Joseph's Early Years

Joseph was the first son born of Jacob (Israel) and his wife Rachel. He was the child of Jacob in his old age and the eleventh of twelve sons. He was greatly valued and highly recognized by his father. Joseph's father favored him over the other children. *"Now Israel loved Joseph more than all his children, because he was the son of his old age: and he made him a coat of many colors"* (Genesis 37:3). Jacob's act of favoritism caused for Joseph to be hated by his brothers. His brothers envied the close relationship their father Jacob had with Joseph. They despised the fact that Joseph received more attention than they were given by their father. This caused much tension in their sibling relationship and as a result, Joseph was at constant odds with his brothers. Genesis 37:4 says, *"And when his brethren saw that their father loved him more than all his brethren, they hated him, and could not speak peaceably unto him.*" Joseph learned through divine dreams that God had a greater plan and purpose for his life. Joseph's two dreams pointed to him rising to a position of prominence and being placed in authority over his brothers and family. At the time Joseph had these two dreams, he did not know how his destiny of greatness would come to pass.

Joseph Had to Mature in Understanding
His Divine Purpose

As a youth, Joseph had a vague understanding of his divine purpose. Through dreams, the Lord revealed that he would one day be exalted to a position of authority over his family. But Joseph's decision to reveal his dreams to jealous and angered brothers, led to a series of short-term tough and challenging circumstances that would later result in many generational spiritual blessings. Joseph's life experience shows that God wants the character of his people to be developed through tough and challenging circumstances. I believe Joseph grew to understand this kingdom principle. During Joseph's early years, he had two dreams of great significance. The first dream involved Joseph and his brothers binding sheaves in the field (see Genesis 37:5-8). Joseph's sheaf arose and stood upright and the sheaves of his brothers gathered around and bowed to his sheaf. Now, think about revealing a dream of this nature to siblings who are already hostile, angry, and embittered. Revealing the contents of this dream did not seek to bring peace to the relationship. As a matter of fact, his brothers became angrier because the dream signified them being under Joseph's authority. *"And his brethren said to him, Shalt thou indeed reign over us? Or shalt thou indeed have dominion over us? And they hated him yet the more for his dreams, and for his words"* (Genesis 37:8). Then, Joseph had a second dream. This dream was similar to the first in that it revealed him being placed in a position of authority over his siblings. In the second dream, the sun, moon, and eleven stars bowed to him. Joseph told his father and brothers this dream. His father reacted by rebuking Joseph. Yet, his brothers' hostility and hatred of Joseph grew deeper. They were determined to get rid of him assuming that by doing so his dreams would not come to pass.

Joseph had some understanding that God would elevate him to prominence but of course, he did not know how or when it would occur. I believe Joseph was excited about his future and in all innocence he unveiled his dreams to his brothers and father. It does not appear as though Joseph intended to anger his brothers by revealing his dreams. Perhaps Joseph was trying to understand the relevance and essence of his dreams. Even his father Jacob had some reservations about the essential message Joseph's second dream conveyed. We know that Jacob pondered or held the interpretation of the second dream close to his heart (see Genesis 37:11). Perhaps due to Joseph's youthfulness and lack of maturity, he may not have understood the importance of allowing his dreams to be revealed at the time appointed by God. Proverbs 12:23a says, *"A prudent man concealeth knowledge..."* In this scripture passage, the word "prudent" means a cautious, wise, and judicious person. A cautious and wise person demonstrates maturity. They understand the importance of reserving the details of their divinely purposed life until the appointed time. Maturity is a process and we don't mature overnight. Maturity comes as a result of consistently living a divinely principled life. Revealing a divine plan ahead of schedule can bring a load of challenges.

Challenges that may have been intended for a future season in our life of faith can be launched prematurely. As in the case of Joseph, when we make a commitment to be devoted to God, he gives us the divine wisdom to overcome every challenge encountered.

Joseph's Character Was Strengthened by Challenges

Joseph is commended for his willingness to remain true to godly principles in spite of his numerous life challenges. Consider the challenges Joseph faced. First, he was sold as a slave by his brothers to the Ishmaelites. His rights as a human being were stripped the moment he was sold. Joseph would experience the pain of separation from his birth family and homeland. He would endure living as a foreigner in Egypt. When someone in Egypt saw Joseph, they knew he was not an Egyptian. His facial features and skin tone reflected that he was of the Hebrew nation. At the time, Egypt was a leading nation and the job of a slave was physically demanding. The Egyptian rulers relied heavily on slave labor to promote their lifestyle of affluence and keep their kingdoms thriving. Yet, Joseph obtained favorable standing with his master and was given opportunities that may have been denied or unavailable to slaves because the Lord was with him. In the most difficult and trying circumstances, it is best to have the Lord with you. When the Lord is with you, you are never alone.

The favor of God rested on the life of Joseph. His master Potiphar noticed that Joseph was different. He entrusted to Joseph the position of overseer. As overseer, Joseph was responsible for all the affairs related to Potiphar's home. Joseph did well as an overseer and Potiphar did not concern himself with the responsibilities under his purview. Joseph could be trusted. He proved to be a man of integrity. Joseph's selection as an overseer shows that you can accomplish much in spite of your surrounding environment or presenting circumstance. You open the door to limitless possibilities, when God's favor rest on your life. His favor is visible and apparent. It will prompt others to acknowledge your gifting or talent and put it to use. As in the case of Joseph, the favor of God in your life makes the notable difference.

Second, Joseph faced the challenge of maintaining a standard of godliness amidst false accusation. Potiphar's wife was attracted to Joseph. She flirted with Joseph, wanting Joseph to become involved in an adulterous relationship. She pestered him night and day. But, in all instances of her sexual advances, Joseph refused to act or behave in a sinful manner. He did not fall prey to her lusts and demands. He upheld God's standard of righteousness and this angered his owner's wife greatly. Joseph says to his owner's wife, *"There is none greater in this house than I; neither hath he kept back anything from me but thee, because thou art his wife: how then can I do this great wickedness, and sin against God"* (Genesis 39:9). She continued to pursue Joseph but Joseph continued to reject her advances. One day, when no other men of the house were present, she caught Joseph by his garment and he fled the home. She took the portion of the garment that remained in her hand to support her fabricated story of Joseph trying to seduce her. The wife's fabricated story resulted in Joseph spending time in a dark Egyptian prison with seemingly no hope of ever being released.

Joseph's imprisonment was not as a result of an unjust or malicious act of crime. He was jailed for doing what was right. Joseph made a decision to follow the principles of God's word and he was jailed. He saw adultery just as it is in the eyes of God, sinful and wicked. Joseph's time in prison did not seem to be the likely path for his life considering that his two dreams pointed to a great future. In spite of his imprisonment, Joseph maintained his integrity and persevered in his faith. We have the biblical record of Joseph doing good while a slave and a prisoner. Joseph even obtained favor with the prison guard. The prison guard entrusted prisoners to Joseph's care. Isn't it ironic that Joseph, a prisoner, was responsible for other prisoners? Time and again, while in Egypt, we see favor being given to Joseph. (I've found that favor allows you to be recognized as one of God's trusted vessels, even in the most difficult situations.) Joseph would later discover that prison would be the place that his divine gift of dream interpretation would be revealed to the Pharaoh of Egypt and result in his promotion. Lastly, Joseph exercised humility in his life as a slave and prisoner. Notice that in both instances in which Joseph was under the authority of Potiphar and the prison guard, he submitted. He did not organize a revolt to escape being jailed. Instead, he patiently endured and was eventually rewarded.

I've worked in the field of human resources for nearly twenty years and colleagues have shared with me instances in which employees experienced harassment and acts of retaliation by management as a result of their refusal to falsify forms, give false statements or support illegal activities. These employees were more concerned about their integrity than the high salaries they were making. They did not follow illegal directives given

by management. They took a stand and in some ca.
them their jobs. Initially, it appears as though the ii
engaged in illegal practices are gaining a greater advant..g̣c than
those not engaged in unlawful deeds. However, this is not the
case. God's way of doing things always triumphs. When we do
things God's way, we win. Those involved in illegal activities
are eventually caught and face public embarrassment and
humiliation. They are penalized and in most cases spend the
remaining portion of their lives dealing with the consequences
of their illegal actions. It is best to act according to the
principles of God's word the first time around.

Let's take a closer look at Joseph's character before and after his
rise to prominence.

Joseph's Character Before and After Rise to Prominence

- Trustworthy (Genesis 39:5–6; 22-23; 41:39-41)
- One of integrity and noble character (Genesis 39:7-9)
- Honest (Genesis 40:12-15; 18-22)
- Forgiving (Genesis 45:1-11; 50:19-21)

From the bulleted list above, we see that Joseph consistently
displayed character before and after his rise to prominence.
Character is demonstrated when we say "yes" to righteousness
and "no" to unrighteousness. Character is displayed each time
we choose to honor God and the principles of his Word over
the attitude, perceptions and thoughts of others. When we
consistently act according to the principles of God's word, we
receive greater blessings in the long run. God does not forget
our righteous deeds. He will expand our sphere of influence.
As modeled in the life of Joseph, God will promote you.
Psalms 75:6,7 tells us, *"For promotion cometh neither from the east, nor*

from the west, nor from the south. But God is the judge: he putteth down one, and setteth up another."

Joseph Learned the Importance of Preparation
Prior to Promotion

Joseph's divine gift of dream interpretation opened the door for him to be promoted by the ruling Pharaoh and his character allowed him to be recognized throughout time as a remarkable leader. Joseph came to the understanding that his enslavement, and the challenges he encountered as a slave in Egypt prepared him for the position he occupied as second to Pharaoh in Egypt. This is evident by Joseph's response to his brothers following the death of their father Jacob. Joseph says, *"Fear not: for am I in the place of God? But, as for you, ye thought evil against me; but God meant it unto good, to bring to pass, as it is this day, to save much people alive"* (Genesis 50:19, 20).

Joseph's brothers were concerned that he would be bitter and resentful towards them for selling him to slave traders. They feared he would exercise vengeance after their father's death and force them to be slaves. But, this was not the heart of Joseph. Joseph demonstrated his unfailing love for God by forgiving his brothers and reassuring them that ultimately God's purpose triumphed through their evil plot. Joseph's act of forgiveness served as a blessing to Joseph as well as his brothers. In the case of Joseph, he was freed from any pain associated with his period of enslavement and his brothers were freed from the burden of resentment and regret associated with selling Joseph.

Joseph Learned to Wait for God's Divine Season of Manifestation

Joseph grew in understanding that the manifestation of God's purpose is based on God's timetable, and not his own. I'm sure Joseph wanted to be released from the Egyptian prison sooner than the appointed time. After all, he did not commit any crime or unjust act that would have warranted a prison sentence. I'm sure if Joseph could choose the time of fulfillment, he may have selected the time period shortly after he interpreted the dream of Pharaoh's chief servant who was released from prison and restored to his position. But, the all-knowing God purposed the divine season in which Joseph would be released from prison and elevated to a position of great authority. In the case of Joseph, he ended up spending two years in prison after his interpretation of the chief servant's dream and the remainder of his life served as a blessing to Egypt, his family, the entire nation of Israel and countless others. God selects the season in which he will fulfill his purpose for our lives. The season of manifestation is determined by God, and not us. Of course, our lack of cooperation with God can cause unnecessary delays. When we cooperate with God, we stay on track with his timing.

Enduring Life Challenges

The life of Joseph was greatly blessed as a result of him enduring the life challenges he encountered. Life challenges can serve as a means whereby our character is developed. In the account of Joseph's life, we learned that Joseph forgave his brothers in spite of the difficulties he faced after being sold as a slave. Joseph remained committed to the Lord and did not give-in to the temptation of adultery with his owner's wife. He utilized his divine gift of dream interpretation after being falsely accused and jailed for his act of righteousness. When the time for his elevation arrived, Joseph was ready to assume the position of second to Pharaoh in the land of Egypt. Joseph's life serves as a testimony to believers that life challenges can bring a greater blessing if we are willing to exercise godliness and endure. Endurance is a fruit of the spirit that some prefer to delay its development. The most preferred life is one free of tests, trials and challenges. But, we are not promised such. Job says, *"Man that is born of a woman is of few days, and full of trouble"* (Job 14:1). The reality this scripture brings to light is a truth some try to shirk. Challenges, tests and trials are certain in life. Jesus our Lord did not live void of life challenges. He had the Pharisees, Sadducees, political leaders and others who doubted or denied his sonship. Jesus had to contend with these groups during his earthly ministry. As believers, we must recognize that we will face life challenges. When we envision life challenges as a building block to our success, we develop greater confidence in God. As demonstrated in the life of Joseph, our character is greatly enhanced when we endure and act godly during challenges. Endurance gives us the ability to maintain God's prescribed standard of righteousness while undergoing life challenges. Make it your determination to view life challenges relative to their eternal significance. When we recognize the positive impact our life challenges have on our eternal reward in heaven, we can rejoice in knowing that the opposition we encountered was well worth it.

Key Principles

1. Character is to be desired and developed.

2. Character demonstrates to others that you highly esteem godly principles and covet the presence of God in your life.

3. A continued pattern of disobedience leads to poor character.

4. A lack of character will result in an unfulfilled life.

Prayer

Heavenly Father, give me your divine understanding that I may successfully navigate life challenges and obstacles. Allow each experience you have purposed for my life build and strengthen my character in Jesus' Name, Amen.

Study Questions for Chapter Two are on pages 154 - 155

Chapter Three

Carnal vs. Spiritual

This I say then, Walk in the Spirit, and ye shall not fulfill the lust of the flesh

Galatians 5:16

The Nature War

There are two natures and one is at war with the other to hinder our spiritual progress. Prior to our faith in Christ, we were led by the dictates of the carnal nature. The carnal nature is the inborn nature we received as a result of our natural or physical birth. This inborn nature was given as a result of the sin of Adam and Eve in the beginning. This nature is rooted in disobedience and rebellion against God. Its passions oppose God. Its desires are contrary to God. Those who live in bondage to the carnal nature, never fulfill their divine purpose.

When we come to faith in Christ, we are no longer in bondage to this inborn nature. We are set free. But, this nature doesn't give up its former rule easily. It fights wanting to regain control over our lives. It seeks to draw us away from the purposes of God. Galatians 5:17 (NIV) says, *"For the sinful [carnal] nature desires what is contrary to the Spirit, and the Spirit what is contrary to the sinful [carnal] nature. They are in conflict with each other, so that you do not do what you want."* This nature is at war with our renewed nature in Christ, and it is incumbent on us to daily put to death the deeds, passions and lusts of this carnal nature. Romans 8:13 says, *"For if you live according to the sinful [carnal] nature, you will die; but if by the Spirit you put to death [crucify, kill, slay, bring to an utter end] the misdeeds of the body, you will live."* We have been given life to its fullest extent by the Spirit of God. Living by the Spirit of God means we allow our renewed nature in Christ to exercise control over the carnal nature. In so doing, we are not making provision for the carnal nature to rule and the will of the Spirit is paramount in our lives.

The Carnal Mind

The carnal mind desires to do that which brings pleasure to the flesh or body. As believers, we are responsible for exercising authority over the dictates of the carnal mind. In his letter to the Romans, the Apostle Paul said the following concerning the carnal mind: *"Because the carnal mind is enmity against God: for it is not subject to the law of God, neither indeed can be"* (Romans 8:7). By nature, the carnal mind despises God. It is inherently rebellious against the nature and character of God. It is not subject to the law of God. Romans 8:5, 6 says, *"For they that are after the flesh do mind the things of the flesh; but they that are after the Spirit the things of the Spirit. For to be carnally minded is death; but to be spiritually minded is life and peace."* Exercising authority over the dictates of the carnal mind requires that we get serious about living a life of faith in Christ Jesus. When we are serious about living for Christ, we will take the necessary steps to ensure that our life of faith is lived as God purposed.

In my walk of faith, I've learned that one way to exercise authority over the dictates of the carnal mind is to maintain a heart ablaze for God. This means sustaining a fiery passion for God. If our heart is not ablaze for God, we are susceptible to experiencing spiritual atrophy. Spiritual atrophy is a condition that has negatively impacted the body of Christ. Similar to muscle atrophy, which is the gradual decline, wasting away, degeneration, or weakening of a muscle as a result of a lack of exercise or paralysis, spiritual atrophy is the weakening of one's zeal, vigor and passion for God as a result of extended periods of ineffectiveness and a lack of direction. It causes many to become "seat warmers" in the local church, not performing actions that are significant and meaningful to the kingdom of

God. The passions of "seat warmers" are formulated based on the growing trends of carnal culture. They take great pleasure in carnal pursuits. They serve as perfect examples of those who either lack the understanding of their divine purpose or the responsibility they hold in making sure their purpose is fulfilled. Do not be a seat warmer. Let your heart continue to be on fire for God.

The Carnal State of the Church at Corinth

First Corinthians is one of two letters that the Apostle Paul writes to the church at Corinth. In First Corinthians, Paul addresses divisions in the church, immorality, and the abuse of Christian freedom. Paul wanted the Corinthian church to get their spiritual lives in order. Continuing in a carnal state would have only crippled the Corinthian church. Corinth was a trade city located between two seas. Approximately 500,000 people lived in Corinth during the time of Paul's emissary work. Merchants and sailors eager to find work in the trade field, migrated to Corinth. Professional gamblers, athletes, and harlots lived in Corinth. Slaves sometimes freed but not having a permanent dwelling place, roamed the streets daily. Moral decadence and freedom of thought was engrained in the culture of Corinth.[4] Paul shared the gospel message with the residents of Corinth and several became converts. Paul's evangelistic efforts led to the establishment of a flourishing church filled with people whose lifestyle once contributed to the moral depravity of the city. These new converts of the Corinthian

---

[4]Herbert Lockyer, Sr. with F.F. Bruce and R.K. Harrison, *Illustrated Dictionary of the Bible*, (Nashville, Tennessee: Thomas Nelson Publishers, 1986).

church would be challenged to live united in Christ though they were formerly from various economic, social, and moral backgrounds. Corinth would seem to be the least likely place for a flourishing body of believers. But, when the gospel message is ministered and lives are changed by the power of God's word, the most unlikely of events occur, including the conversion of those who were once living contrary to God's standard of living. Paul spent time in Corinth teaching the Word of God to the Corinthian church (see Acts 18:11, 18). A period of time after Paul's departure, it was reported to him that there were divisions in the church at Corinth (see I Corinthians 1:11). Some claimed to be followers of Paul, others Apollos and Cephas. This created disharmony. Paul points out their error and provides understanding. He reminds them that they are one in Christ Jesus. They were united in Christ by the preaching of the cross. The Corinthian followers' birth into the kingdom of God was based on Christ's death, burial and resurrection. Their oneness in Christ put an end to divisions. In Paul's epistle to the Corinthian church he describes them as being "carnal".

According to I Corinthians chapter 3, carnal also signifies:

- An infant phase of growth in the Christian faith
- Spiritual immaturity

The infancy phase in Christ can be categorized as the beginning phase of one's new life in Jesus Christ. The terms *newborn, new creature* or *new creation* are used interchangeably in the New Testament to denote a person's entrance into a brand new life in Jesus Christ. The infancy phase requires gaining a solid understanding of God's word and maturing in salvation. Without a solid understanding of God's word, the new believer can become persuaded by various teachings that are not biblical. Metaphorically, the growth process of the new believer parallels the infant growth process. An infant is born with a stomach the size of a marble. At about ten days of age, the stomach is the size of a ping-pong ball. The stomach steadily increases in size as the infant grows. The stomach becomes more elastic, allowing the infant to consume more milk and later solid foods.

As a parent, I've witnessed the infant growth process in the lives of our children. As infants, our children's diet consisted of milk or infant formula without any additions for the first four months of life. My husband and I have concluded that our son's desire for milk far superseded the girls. When our son cried he exerted as much force as humanly possible from his lungs, to signal his hunger for milk. Thankfully, we were loving parents and considered it a pleasure to meet not only our son's need but the need of our girls. As their daily intake of milk or infant formula reached the American Pediatric Academy recommended peak of 30 ounces, we began to introduce solid foods into their diet. The solid foods they were fed included infant rice cereal, infant oatmeal, and pureed fruits and vegetables. Then, around nine to twelve months we began to introduce them to "junior" foods. These foods were slightly coarser than pureed foods and required more chewing. We also began to include foods such as mashed potatoes, sweet potatoes, and yogurt. Once the baby reached a point of self-feeding, table food became the standard diet. And, the baby lacked interest in pureed or junior foods. There was no turning back to the basics. Notice that the infant had to gradually progress from a diet that primarily consisted of milk or infant formula, to pureed baby foods and infant cereal, to junior foods and finally table foods. Similarly, the new believer in Christ goes through a growth process. During the early phase of salvation, there is an innate spiritual hunger for the Word. This hunger must be fed by biblical based teaching and preaching that aids in establishing foundational knowledge of God's word. Then, as the new believer continues to grow, they graduate to a point where they are able to receive messages that contain deeper, spiritual meaning. This is not an overnight process and requires diligence on the part of the believer and those committed to their discipleship in Christ. On the other hand, if the new believer's hunger for the Word of God is not fed, they will become spiritually malnourished and completely ineffective. They may also abandon their faith in Christ.

We get a sense of the Apostle Paul's sentiments toward the Corinthian church when he says, *"And I, brethren, could not speak unto you as unto spiritual, but as unto carnal, even as unto babes in Christ. I have fed you with milk, and not with meat: for hitherto ye were not able to bear it, neither yet now are ye able"* (I Corinthians 3:1, 2). Notice how Paul uses the terms "milk" and "meat" to describe the faith message. Milk tends to denote simple, foundational, elementary teachings of the faith. Meat tends to denote deeper, more complex mysteries of the faith. Milk is designed for those who are new converts and growing in the understanding of salvation. Meat is designed for those who have matured beyond elementary teachings and possess the spiritual maturity to comprehend a deeper message. Paul knew that ministering a message fitted for a spiritually mature audience would not be conducive to the young, infant spiritual diet of the Corinthians. However, when we examine Paul's response in the later part of verse 2, I think Paul had greater expectations of the Corinthian church. I believe Paul was also disappointed with the spiritual state of affairs at the Corinthian church after his departure for in the later part of I Corinthians 3, verse 2, Paul points out that the Corinthian church was not able to bear a more spiritual message. Paul was unable to share with the Corinthian church a message that contained deeper spiritual truths because of their carnality. I can only imagine the disappointment Paul must have experienced after discovering that the church he pioneered had not matured beyond infancy. I'm sure he expected the Corinthian church to be farther along in their walk of faith. Unfortunately, this was not the case.

The Corinthian church fell into the unfortunate trap, as some do, of allowing their actions and thoughts to be governed by their carnal nature. This greatly reduced their effectiveness as believers and inhibited their growth in Christ. We must not make any provision for the carnal nature to rule. Believers are challenged with growing to the point that our (godly) actions are perfectly consistent with our (godly) thoughts. If we live less than this, we are giving the carnal nature an opportunity to show its ugliness. Furthermore, we are sending a mixed message to the unbelieving world.

The Spiritual Mind

The spiritual mind seeks to please God and is life and peace. As born again believers, we have been given life through the spirit of God. The spiritual mind is in total agreement with God. The spiritual mind is focused on the initiatives of heaven and bringing those initiatives to pass in the earth. In Romans 12:2, we are instructed to be transformed by the renewing of our mind. Romans 12:2b (NIV) says, *"Do not conform any longer to the pattern of this world, but be transformed by the renewing of your mind."*

The transformation of our mind requires effort and work on our part. The mind has to be trained and disciplined. Without training and discipline, the mind is like a wandering wild beast. What can we do to renew the mind? One, be determined to not allow the carnal mind to rule. This means we will not be controlled or led by carnal thoughts. Philippians 4:8 tells us, *"Finally, brethren, whatsoever things are true, whatsoever things are honest, whatsoever things are just, whatsoever things are pure, whatsoever things are lovely, whatsoever things are of good report; if there be any virtue, and if there be any praise, think on these things"*. When we saturate our minds with the thoughts outlined in Philippians 4:8, we are training the mind to think and focus on godly thoughts. This results in a healthy mind. An unhealthy mind can lead to an unproductive life. The Bible tells us that as you think within yourself, so are you (see Proverbs 23:7). Our thought life is very important. An unhealthy thought life can lead to a fruitless life.

Another way we can renew the mind is to make a decision to live according to our identity in Christ. The believers' identity is not based on perceptions held by others, societal or cultural trends. If we do not know who we are in Christ, the enemy will seize the opportunity to capitalize on our ignorance and unleash his schemes that are designed to keep our understanding darkened. Our understanding must be enlightened with the truth of God's eternal word. II Corinthians 5:17 says, *"Therefore if any man [woman] be in Christ, he is a new creature: Old things are passed away; Behold, all things are become new."* We are a new creation. A new creation is a brand new being created in the image of Christ Jesus. This transformation is to be evident to others by our actions, deeds, and speech. If we not understand that we are a brand new creation in Christ, we become a primary target for the enemy and are subject to live according to the dictates of the carnal mind.

We are citizens of God's kingdom. The rights, privileges and benefits of our kingdom citizenship extend far beyond our natural citizenship. I Peter 2:9 says, *"But ye are a chosen generation, a royal priesthood, a holy nation, a peculiar people; that ye should shew forth the praises of him who hath called you out of darkness into his marvelous light."* We are a select or chosen generation. We are chosen by God to be a representative of his kingdom in the earth. We are a royal priesthood. This honorable distinction is given to us as citizens of God's kingdom and can only be received when we put our faith in Christ for our salvation. Glory to God! We are a part of a heavenly royal family where Jesus rules, lives, and reigns. No earthly royal family can compete with our heavenly royal status. We are a holy nation. We are set a part from the filth, corruption and sin prevalent in our world. We are a peculiar people. We belong to God. Our entire being belongs to him. We are God's property.

We are God's workmanship or masterpiece to the world. We have been created in Christ Jesus to do good works. Ephesians 2:10 says, *"For we are his workmanship, created in Christ Jesus unto good works, which God hath before ordained that we should walk in them."* When you examine the history of this verse, the Apostle Paul was writing to the church at Ephesus. This church was comprised of Gentiles who came to faith in Christ (see Ephesians 3:1). The Gentile nation did not have a good reputation amongst the Jews. They were known to be pagan worshippers, immoral, unjust and just plain heathenistic. They were once estranged from the covenant promises and blessings of God. In verse 10, Paul was saying to the church at Ephesus, look at who you are. They were God's masterpiece. They had been created in Christ Jesus to do good works, not the evil, destructive and damaging works they were once accustomed when their life was under the authority of the enemy. I'm sure the church at Ephesus was infused with a greater degree of grace after reading Paul's letter. They could envision themselves as being God's master work of art and live according to this truth.

We are overcomers and have overcome the world through the exercising of our faith. I John 5:4 which says, *"For whatsoever is born of God <u>overcometh</u> the world: and this is the victory that overcometh the world, even our faith."* God has given us the power to exercise authority over the world, the world's system and its practices. We are overcomers in Christ Jesus.

We are the <u>sons</u> and <u>daughters</u> <u>of God</u>. I John 3:1 says, *"Behold, what manner of love the Father hath bestowed upon us, that we should be called the sons [daughters] of God: therefore the world knoweth us not, because it knew him not."* No earthly love can measure to the love the Father has for us. There isn't a greater or better father than God. There are countless references in scripture of who we are in Christ. As we live according to our identity in Christ, we are allowing the personhood of Jesus Christ to resonate and the fulfillment of our divine purpose is inevitable.

Key Principles

1. If we live by the spirit of God, we will not fulfill the passions and desires of the carnal nature.

2. Continually following the dictates of the carnal mind will result in a wasted, unproductive life.

3. The inherent nature of the carnal mind is to oppose the nature and character of God.

4. The spiritual mind is life and peace in God.

Prayer

Lord, thank you for your grace to live by the spirit of God. My carnal nature no longer rules or controls my life. I have been set free to live as you have purposed. As I consistently take steps to renew my mind, let my transformation serve as a beacon of light to others in Jesus' name, Amen.

Study Questions for Chapter Three are on page 156

Chapter Four

Spiritual Warfare

For we wrestle not against flesh and blood, but against principalities, against powers, against the rulers of the darkness of this world, against spiritual wickedness in high places.

Ephesians 6: 12

What is Spiritual Warfare?

Spiritual warfare is a reality in the life of every believer. We will encounter and experience warfare throughout our journey of faith. Spiritual warfare is the battle between the kingdom of God and the kingdom of darkness. The kingdom of darkness desires to destroy the believer before the accomplishment of God's will in the earth. Jesus revealed the mission of the enemy and the kingdom of darkness. Jesus says, *"The thief cometh not, but for to steal, and to kill, and to destroy..."* (John 10:10a). In the Old Testament, warfare was characterized as armed conflict between Israel (God's covenant people) and pagan groups of people. These pagan groups were enemies of Israel and desired to destroy them. When Israel consulted God and followed his instructions, they were victorious over their enemies. But, when Israel turned from serving God and began living just as their pagan enemies, they suffered defeat.

Spiritual warfare serves as a reminder of our need for God's divine intervention to live an overcoming and victorious life. We must continually seek the Lord to overcome obstacles and progressively grow in faith. If progressive growth is not a part of the Christian experience, we are destined to become comfortable and lack the essential characteristics of being effective for the kingdom of God. Our divine purpose will not be fulfilled. The Promised Land was not a place of comfort, relaxation or ease. The Israelites had to engage in war and fight many battles against their enemies. When our nation engages in war, leading military authorities come together to formulate a plan of action that is designed to bring victory. Soldiers do not enter combat without having a strategy or plan of action.

Professional sports teams are serious about winning and being a star team. Coaches spend countless hours developing and formulating strategies to beat the opponent. The enemy is our opponent and he is cunning. He has been devising plans of destruction for eons of time. He wants to destroy the plan of God for our lives. If he could have his way in our lives, he would make sure we would not be what God has destined for us to be. In order to fulfill our divine purpose, we must engage in spiritual warfare. We cannot allow the enemy's plan of destruction and defeat for our lives to prevail. We must be prepared to defeat the enemy.

Weapons of Warfare

Spiritual warfare requires the use of *spiritual* weapons to be victorious over the enemy. *"(For the weapons of our warfare are not carnal, but mighty through God to the pulling down of strong holds ;) Casting down imaginations, and every high thing that exalteth itself against the knowledge of God, and bringing into captivity every thought to the obedience of Christ"* (2 Corinthians 10:4). Carnal in this scripture passage is a reference to strategies, concepts, or ideas that are predicated on sensual, worldly reasoning. The weapons we employ in warfare are not predicated on sensual and worldly reasoning for these are limited in scope and do not have their origin in God. Their basis is not consistent with the nature of God and does not seek to promote the purposes of God's Kingdom.

The weapons of our warfare are spiritual in nature and possess the power of God to defeat demonic powers, forces, and rulers of darkness. The weapons we employ are effective, bringing an end to the enemy's plan. Some of these weapons are prayer, fasting, and the Word of God. These weapons are effective in strengthening our faith, birthing God's purposes, and destroying the plan of the enemy.

The Weapon of Prayer

Prayer is an effective weapon to employ in warfare. Prayer will be discussed in greater depth in Chapter Six. But, I will provide an overview of prayer relative to its importance to spiritual warfare. Prayer is mandatory and not optional in warfare. Prayer intercepts the tactics of the enemy and bring to ruin his plans of destruction.

During spiritual warfare, prayer gives power to angels to minister on our behalf and help usher victory. Concerning angels, *Hebrews 1:14 says, "Are they not all ministering spirits, sent forth to minister for them who shall be heirs of salvation?"* Angels have been given a charge to minister to us. When we are engaged in spiritual warfare, angels are dispatched to come to our aid. Scripture gives the account of angels being sent to assist Peter after being jailed for his labor in spreading the message of Jesus Christ. The early church experienced intense spiritual warfare with satanic forces that operated through political and religious leaders to hinder the spread of the gospel message. Peter played an instrumental role in the spread of the gospel in the region of Jerusalem. When the early church followers received news that Peter had been jailed, they began to pray fervently for God's divine intervention. Acts 12:5b says, *"... But prayer was made without ceasing of the church unto God for him."* James had just been martyred for his faith and role in spreading the gospel. Early church followers did not want Peter to be killed. While they were praying, an angel of the Lord was sent to release Peter from prison. Peter thought he was having a vision but this was not the case. Peter's release from prison was an unexpected miraculous act of God fueled by the weapon of prayer. When Peter knocked on the door of the gate where the early church followers were praying, the young woman who answered heard his voice. She was so excited to see him that she did not open the gate to allow his entry. Instead, she reported to the early church followers that Peter was outside the gate. The early church followers thought she had lost her soberness of mind. But, she continued to tell her story. They supposed she saw Peter's angel and not Peter at the gate. Peter continued to knock and when they opened the door and saw him, they were amazed. Peter had to assure them that he had been miraculously set free by an angel of the Lord. Peter's miraculous release from prison is a demonstration of the tremendous power that is unleashed from heaven when the weapon of prayer is used in warfare.

The Weapon of Fasting

Fasting is an important discipline in the Christian faith. Fasting helps to consecrate the heart and mind so that we are focused on fulfilling God's intended purposes. Fasting is one of the primary keys to victory during a period of spiritual warfare. When we examine the lives of the Israelites, fasting was a common practice especially during periods of warfare. When Israel needed to get instructions from the Lord on how to exercise victory over their enemies, they devoted themselves to fasting.

There are three commonly practiced ways of fasting: total abstinence from food and drink, abstinence from food only, and restricted dietary practices. In scripture, we have the example of Queen Esther who directed all the Israelites impacted by the king's edict to be killed, to fast, not consuming food or drink for three days and nights (see Esther 4:16). After the three day period of abstinence from food and drink, Esther risked her life by approaching the king. Her efforts helped to save the people from annihilation. Jesus during a period of temptation in the wilderness abstained from food for a period of forty days. Afterwards, he returned in the power of the Spirit to Galilee (see Luke 4: 1 -14). And, lastly Daniel who committed to fast twenty-one days or three weeks by abstaining from pleasant bread, meat or drink. Also, he did not use any oils to hydrate his skin (see Daniel 10:3) during his period of abstinence from tasty foods, meat or drink. After his twenty-one days of fasting, the angel of the Lord revealed to him that the answer he sought of God was released the day he commissioned to fast. But, a demonic force, the prince of the kingdom of Persia, withstood the angel twenty one days and the angel was rescued, bringing Daniel the response he sought. In the aforementioned examples, it is evident that fasting resulted in the people of God receiving the answer sought or the spiritual breakthrough desired. Throughout the life of a believer, one if not all of these ways of fasting are used in drawing near to the Lord and are keys to victory during spiritual warfare.

The fast that is chosen by God brings him glory and results in many blessings. Isaiah 58:6 points out some of the blessings of fasting. These blessings include: the loosing of the band of wickedness, reversing heavy burdens, setting the oppressed free and breaking every yoke. These blessings are manifested when we fast according to God's prescribed plan.

Fasting can be done corporately by a local church or body of believers unified on a single purpose. Or, fasting can be done individually. Whether fasting is done corporately or individually, it is to be done willingly. It is important to remember that when you decide to fast, remain true to your commitment and fast with the understanding that your *primary* purpose is to draw closer to the Lord and create an atmosphere in which you can hear clearly from him.

The Word of God as a Weapon of Defense

Jesus experienced spiritual warfare during his earthly ministry. The forty days Jesus spent in the wilderness while being tempted of the devil was a period of spiritual warfare and he used the Word of God as a weapon of defense. Luke 4:1 - 13 gives the account of Jesus being tempted by the devil while in the wilderness. In reading this account, you will notice how the enemy comes in varying forms to distort the truth of God's Word. While in the wilderness, the first temptation the enemy presented to Jesus related to food. Interesting as Jesus was *fasting* during his time in the wilderness. *"And the devil said unto him, If thou be the Son of God, command this stone that it be made bread"* (Luke 4:3). The devil was tempting Jesus to prove his sonship by turning the stone into bread. Jesus, knowing that He is the Son of God, countered the temptation by speaking the Word. Jesus said, *"It is written, that man shall not live by bread alone but by every word of God"* (Luke 4:4). Jesus lived by the word of God. He never deviated from his Father's word. So, when the tempter presented this identity ploy, Jesus used the word of God as a weapon of defense. We must have the same steadfastness and commitment to live by God's Word as Jesus.

If we want to have a successful life in Christ and have victory during a period of warfare, we must live by God's Word. The Old Testament parallel scripture to Luke 4:3 is Deuteronomy 8:3b. In the Deuteronomy scripture passage, the Lord was instructing Israel to follow all the commands He had given them so that they would live, prosper, and possess the Promised Land. Similarly, as God's people, we must follow His Word if we want to live, have a prosperous life and possess the promises God has made available to us through faith in Jesus Christ. Fulfilling our divine purpose involves appropriating the promises of God.

The second temptation the devil presented to Jesus involved worship. The enemy promised to give Jesus all the kingdoms of the world, authority and power if he worshipped him. As in the first temptation, Jesus used the word of God to combat the enemy and did not give-in to his demands. Jesus answered, *"For it is written, thou shalt worship the Lord thy God, and him only shalt thou serve"* (Luke 4:8b). God alone is to be worshipped. Our love and devotion is to be to the Lord. Time and again, in each temptation the enemy presented, Jesus responded by declaring the truth of God's word. Jesus said, *"It is said, thou shalt not tempt the Lord thy God"* (Luke 4:12). Notice that in all three temptations, we learn the importance of knowing, understanding and declaring God's word. Hebrews 4:12 says, *"For the Word of God is quick, and powerful, and sharper than any two edged sword, piercing even to the diving asunder of soul and spirit, and of the joints and marrow, and is a discerner of the thoughts and intents of the heart."* The word of God is a powerful weapon to use in warfare. When we commit to speak the truth of God's word, just as Jesus our Lord, we are victorious over the enemy.

Seek the Heart of the Lord

Seeking the heart of the Lord is a requirement during a time of warfare. The enemy wages war at a time when you are diligently seeking the heart of God with the intent of bringing frustration and hopelessness. Seeking the heart of the Lord involves becoming single in focus and purpose to request, petition or ask the Lord for direction through sincere prayer. Psalms 34:10 reads, *"The young lions do lack, and suffer hunger: but they that seek the Lord shall not want any good thing"*. This is a great and precious promise. While a young lion may not be skilled at catching its prey for food, as the experienced lion, and as a result suffers hunger, you will <u>not</u> suffer lack. This means you will not be without understanding when you seek the Lord. God promised to provide you with what is needed.

Let's examine the blessings that were imparted to King Jehoshaphat and the people of Judah as a result of them seeking the Lord during a period of warfare. His name was Jehoshaphat (juh HAH shuh fat), quite the tongue twister with respect to pronunciation, but he was a king filled with godly wisdom. His faith in God proved to be a blessing to him as well as the people of Judah. During his kingship, he attacked pagan idolatry and sent teachers to teach the people about God as the people did not have individual scrolls for their reference. We are blessed today with the convenience of purchasing bibles or accessing bible applications by way of technology for our individual reference and use. In affairs of the state, Jehoshaphat demonstrated a willingness to rely on the Lord. He knew that if he sought the heart of the Lord, he would receive the answer needed. Jehoshaphat's faith in the Lord led him to delight in the ways of the Lord. He had high regard for

God's Word and following the way of the Lord. This means his daily life exemplified godliness. During his reign, the enemies of Judah formed a coalition with the intent of defeating them in war. The coalition forces consisted of the Moabites and the Ammonites. Both nations were great antagonist of Israel. Knowing that the odds were stacked against Israel, Jehoshaphat sought the Lord for strategy and instruction through sincere prayer. In addition to prayer, he declared a fast throughout all of Judah and encouraged the people to seek the Lord diligently for strategy and instruction.

Jehoshaphat's approach to seeking the heart of God through sincere prayer was simple: first, he acknowledged God as the God of their fathers (see 2 Chronicles 20:6). God sovereignly selected Jehoshaphat's forefathers to be representatives of his glory in the earth. He was a descendant of Father Abraham, his son Isaac, and Jacob. God spoke great promises into the lives of his forefathers and many blessings were given to them because of their trust in God. Perhaps, Jehoshaphat could be encouraged by the spiritual legacy of his forefathers. If God blessed them for their faith in his spoken promises, then God would bless him and the people of Judah.

Second, he acknowledged God's sovereignty and power (see 2 Chronicles 20:6). This acknowledgement helps to establish a godly perspective concerning the greatness of God and his awesome power. When Jesus taught the disciples to pray, he said they are to acknowledge God as Father. Jesus says, *"After this manner therefore pray ye: Our Father which art in heaven, Hallowed be thy name"* (St. Matthew 6:9). The disciples were to remember the nature of their relationship with God and know that it is the Father's desire to grant their request. They were to reverence God and acknowledge his holiness. As new covenant believers, it is important that when we approach God, we reverence God and acknowledge Him as the all-powerful, holy God. This is a key element of faith. We must also believe that God will reward us when we commit to passionately pursue Him. He desires to grant the petitions and requests we ask of Him in faith. *"And this is the confidence that we have in him, that, if we ask any thing according to his will, he heareth us: And if we know that he hear us, whatsoever we ask, we know that we have the petitions that we desired of him"* (I John 5:14, 15).

Third, Jehoshaphat put God in remembrance of His delivering power and the promised inheritance of God's people (see 2 Chronicles 20:7). One of the most noted miracles of the Old Testament is God delivering the Israelites from Egyptian bondage and parting the Red Sea, enabling them to journey to freedom on dry land. The miracle of deliverance resulted in other nations acknowledging that the God of the Israelites is the God of Heaven. In addition to deliverance, God promised that he would give the Israelites a promised land for their dwelling. In Jehoshaphat's petition before the Lord, He reminded the Lord of his delivering power. No doubt Jehoshaphat recalled the law, the words spoken by the prophets, or the miraculous conquests of the judges that reaffirmed God's covenant relationship with Israel. The challenge of putting God in remembrance of his mercy, miraculous acts, and promises is given to believers to take on. The all-powerful and all-knowing God doesn't experience a lapse in memory that leads to the failure to recall a past action, event, or occurrence. Reminding God of his delivering power and his promise is for our benefit, not God's. Our faith is strengthened and it gives God reason to intervene on our behalf. The people of God gathered at the temple while Jehoshaphat prayed concerning the planned military attack of the Moabites and the Ammonites. We can learn a lesson from the actions of Jehoshaphat and the people of Judah. When church leadership and laity make a commitment to unite in prayer, we will see God move in miraculous ways.

Lastly, Jehoshaphat asked the Lord to execute judgment on the Moabites and the Ammonites (see 2 Chronicles 20: 10 - 12). In his petition to the Lord, Jehoshaphat recalls of how the Lord did not allow Israel to invade the territory of the Moabites and the Ammonites during their wilderness pilgrimage. The Lord was gracious to the Moabites and the Ammonites, allowing them to remain in their dwelling place and not be destroyed by Israel. It would have been in their best interest to formulate and maintain a friendship with Israel. Instead, they sought to destroy Israel. When the enemy attacks, you have a right to ask God to exercise judgment in the circumstance or ordeal. We should ask for God's fair and righteous judgment in our ordeal. In some cases, God's judgment will require us exercising a greater degree of responsibility but it is best for our spiritual growth and success.

The Power of Prophecy

Prophecy is used by God to give insight into the future. God reveals strategies for defeating the plans of the enemy through prophecy. In the case of Jehoshaphat, after he prayed to the Lord, the Spirit of the Lord came upon the Levite Jahaziel and he began to speak the message the Lord sent from heaven. Jahaziel says, *"Ye shall not need to fight in this battle: set yourselves, stand ye still, and see the salvation of the Lord with you, O Judah and Jerusalem: fear not, nor be dismayed; tomorrow go out against them: for the Lord will be with you"* (2 Chronicles 20:17). His words of prophecy provided relief, comfort, instruction, and strategy to God's people.

Through prophecy, God revealed the next step Judah would take to enforce the victory the Lord had given. Also, through these prophetic words, we come to learn a key principle in spiritual warfare – the battle we fight against the enemy is not ours but the Lord's. When the enemy launches an attack against you, in actuality he is launching an attack against the Lord and his kingdom. The Lord steps-in, intervenes and uses us as instruments of righteousness to execute his divine will. Praise God! We are executing God's divine judgment on the enemy and his cohorts who seek to hinder and destroy the plan of God from being manifested in our lives, when we engage in spiritual warfare.

Prophecy plays a key role in the body of Christ. In the New Testament church, prophecy warns, provides insight into the future, brings comfort and provides direction. The Apostle Paul laid a charge to his spiritual son Timothy by saying, *"This charge I commit unto thee, son Timothy, according to the prophecies which went before on thee, that thou by them mightest war a good warfare;"* (I Timothy 1:18). The Apostle Paul was letting Timothy know that the prophecies spoken over his life can be used as an effective tool for warfare. Paul was exhorting Timothy to not forget the prophetic words spoken. I believe Paul wanted Timothy to remember these words and remain committed to fulfilling his ministry. He did not want Timothy to become stagnant. Stagnation is a lurking reality that attempts to creep into the heart of a believer. We must be aware of its desire to sap the motivation out of us, attempting to prevent us from contending for the faith. "... *Ye should earnestly contend for the faith which was once delivered unto the saints*" (Jude 3). We should not be stagnant in our faith but in a state of continual growth and development so that we become and fulfill that which God has predestined. Has a prophecy been spoken to you? Does that prophecy confirm what God has placed in your heart and align with scripture? If so, you can take that prophecy and use it as a weapon in warfare to defeat the enemy.

Give Praise to God

Judah was led to victory over their enemies through praise. King Jehoshaphat appointed singers to praise the beauty of God's holiness as they went out before the army. The singers declared the glory and power of the Lord. God sent ambushes against their enemies as the singers began singing and praising God. Their enemies were defeated and destroyed when they began praising the Lord. "*As they [the singers of Judah] began to sing and praise, the Lord sent ambushes against the men of Ammon and Moab and Mount Seir who were invading Judah, and they were defeated. When the men of Judah came to the place that overlooks the desert and looked toward the vast army, they saw only dead bodies lying on the ground; no one escaped*" (2 Chronicles 20: 22, 24 NIV). Praise put an end of the plans of Judah's enemies.

Praise is an expression of gratitude to God in response to his goodness and awesomeness. The Word of God says, "*Praise ye the Lord: for it is good to sing praises unto our God; for it is pleasant; and praise is comely*" (Psalms 147:1). The believer should not be coerced to praise God. The believer should instinctively offer praise to God for his eternal sovereignty.

Recognize the Enemy as a Defeated Opponent

Another key to victory during spiritual warfare is recognizing the enemy as a defeated opponent. One of the most glaring examples in the Old Testament of spiritual warfare is the battle between the shepherd boy David and the giant Goliath. David was sent on assignment by his father to give his brothers food and check their status. His brothers enlisted in King Saul's army and were fighting against the Philistines, Israel's adversary. While on assignment, David heard the insults and intimidating speech of the giant Goliath who threatened the army of Israel and King Saul for a period of forty days. Each time Goliath hurled an insult, the army of Israel would draw back in fear. The army of Israel had the power to silence the giant Goliath but they did not use it. Instead, they allowed Goliath to hurl insults and threats for forty days.

David observed their actions and inquired of the reward to be given to the one who would put an end to the giant. David's inquiry is proof that he recognized Goliath as a defeated enemy. David says, *"… For who is this uncircumcised Philistine, that he should defy the armies of the living God?"* (I Samuel 17:26). David was not intimidated by Goliath's size or threatening statements. David saw Goliath as someone he was given authority by God to defeat. Similarly, we must not be intimidated by the enemy or his threats. We must believe that we have been given authority over the enemy since Jesus defeated him at Calvary. So, David spoke with Saul, and after being fitted for Saul's armor only to find that it wasn't designed for his personal use, was given permission to fight Goliath, using his own weaponry. David's armor was a sling and five smooth stones. One would conclude that there was no way David could defeat the giant using such simple weaponry. *"And he [David] took his staff in his hand, and chose him five smooth stones out of the brook, and put them in a shepherd's bag which he had, even in a scrip; and his sling was in his hand: and he drew near to the Philistine"* (I Samuel 17:40). In spiritual warfare, you must put a stop to the enemy's taunting and insults. Put a stop to him promptly so that he does not gain an advantage. We cannot defeat the enemy in our own strength. Just as David, we must ask for God's divine intervention and rely on his supernatural strength for victory.

Do Not Fear

Fear brings torment and will cause for the plans of God to be forfeited. *I John 4:18 says, "There is no fear in love; but perfect love casteth out fear: because fear hath torment. He that feareth is not made perfect in love."* In spiritual warfare, we must not fear. Fear is not of God. Fear provides the enemy with an opportunity to gain an upper hand and results in us being powerless. Fear can be paralyzing and hinder us from taking action against the attack of the enemy. The actions of the prophet Elisha shows the importance of not fearing during warfare.

According to II Kings 6:8, the king of Syria was at war with the nation of Israel. The king of Syria sought to conquer Israel's territories and destroy them. As typical of an enemy, he devised war strategies and commissioned his soldiers to setup camp in various places. But, each time the Syrian soldiers setup camp in a particular place, Elisha sent a messenger to notify the king of Israel of their exact location. There were no secrets this army could keep from the prophet Elisha. God gave Elisha keen insight into the plans of Israel's enemy. Can you imagine having the preciseness and accuracy of Elisha in the prophetic realm of ministry? Elisha's preciseness and accuracy enhanced his credibility with the king of Israel who considered him a trusted and reliable source. Israel's king listened and followed the instructions of Elisha. His insight resulted in Israel gaining a considerable advantage over their Syrian enemies. The king of Syria was forced to call his officers together to find out what was going on. He was certain that someone in his army was betraying him and revealing secrets to Israel. He was angered that he could not gain an advantage over the armies of Israel. Then, one of his officers told him that the prophet Elisha was telling of their whereabouts. His officer also noted that Elisha revealed the words he spoke in the privacy of his bedroom. Syria's king was outraged. He suspended his mission of attacking the army of Israel and focused all of his efforts on capturing and apprehending one fearless man of God, Elisha. He ordered horses, chariots and a strong force to surround the city where Elisha lived. Now, imagine a whole army surrounding a city to apprehend one person. Elisha's servant awakened early in the morning and reported to Elisha that he saw a Syrian army with horses and chariots surrounding the city where they lived. Fear and anxiety began to creep into the heart of his servant. He probably rationalized that there was no way one or two men could defeat an entire army. Fear is deceptive. It distorts the reality of the spiritual realm. It causes for us to focus on the limitations of the physical realm and discard the limitless possibilities in the spiritual realm. Elisha answered his servant and said, *"Fear not: for they that be with us are more than they that be with them"* (2 Kings 6:16). After Elisha told his servant to not fear, he prayed to the Lord and asked that his servants' eyes be opened to see the innumerable heavenly army that surrounded them providing protection. This army could only be seen with the eyes of one's spirit. When we do not fear, we are allowing God to open our spiritual eyes to see heaven's intervention during the enemy's attack. From a logical standpoint, Elisha would have every reason to be fearful as the army that pursued greatly outnumbered him. But, Elisha knew that God's protective provision surrounded them and was far greater than their enemy. Similarly, we must be confident that if God is for us, he is greater than the enemy fighting against us. Romans 8:31 tells us, *"If God be for us, who can be against us?"*

Share Your Testimony

The breakthrough we receive following a period of spiritual warfare should not be a secret. We should share our testimony. Be willing to share with others the weapons of warfare you used or the strategies you employed to exercise victory over the enemy. Each time you share your testimony, you are planting a seed of faith. Others are encouraged to fight during warfare, not give up and make strides toward the fulfillment of their divine purpose. Never underestimate the value of sharing your testimony. It just might be the key to someone's victory.

Key Principles

1. Spiritual warfare cannot be avoided. We will encounter and engage in spiritual warfare.

2. Spiritual warfare should not be shunned. It is to be embraced and accepted as a part of our journey of faith.

3. The enemy is cunning and has been devising schemes for eons of time. We must be alert and prepared to employ the weapons of warfare to defeat the enemy.

4. We are victorious when we apply the weapons of warfare. The weapons of warfare are powerful.

Prayer

Heavenly Father, grant me your divine insight for spiritual warfare. I declare that the schemes and tactics the enemy has deployed against me will not prosper. I am victorious over the enemy. Thank you for imparting divine wisdom to defeat the enemy, in Jesus' name, Amen.

Study Questions for Chapter Four are on page 157

Chapter Five

Wilderness Seasons

Cast not away therefore your confidence, which hath great recompense of reward. For ye have need of patience, that, after ye have done the will of God, ye might receive the promise.

Hebrews 10: 35, 36

Wilderness seasons can be characterized as periods of time between the revealed or known promise of God and the manifestation of the promise. Wilderness seasons require patience and demand greater intimacy with the Lord. These seasons are designed to prepare us for the fulfillment of our divine purpose. Subsequent to salvation and early in our walk of faith, we experience a wilderness season primarily for our foundational development in the Christian faith. The purpose of the wilderness season subsequent to salvation is to prompt growth in our relationship with Jesus Christ. Heaven's desires are birthed in our hearts and we undergo a spiritual transformation. We have a hunger for knowing, understanding and applying God's Word. Throughout our journey of faith, we will experience wilderness seasons. When you closely examine the lives of various biblical characters, you will notice that they did not volunteer for a wilderness season. Wilderness seasons were engrafted into their life of faith. They had to live by faith and believe that God would accomplish what he intended.

When examining the history of the nation of Israel, it is evident that they experienced wilderness seasons. After their deliverance from Egyptian bondage, the Israelites encountered a wilderness season. It is chronicled in scripture of their journey through the wilderness region while traveling to the Promised Land. Their journey was not limited to a geographical wilderness but included a spiritual wilderness season. The Israelites' wilderness season was designed to deepen their faith in the one and true living God who delivered them from bondage. The wilderness season also unveiled several hidden heart issues of the nation of Israel some including unbelief or a lack of faith, stubbornness, and an unwillingness to trust God.

Their spiritual dullness resulted in them being confined to a cycle of rebellion. It is unfortunate that their journey to the Promised Land was prolonged and the generation freed from bondage did not enter the Promised Land as God had purposed.

Wilderness Seasons Deepen the Understanding of Your Divine Purpose

Wilderness seasons help to deepen the understanding of your divine purpose. Let's examine the life of Moses and how he came into the understanding of his divine purpose. God ordained that the prophet Moses, who was born during the period in which the ruling Pharaoh issued an edict to kill every male Israelite boy, serve as Israel's leader and deliverer. Hidden by his parents for approximately three months following his birth, Moses was placed in a floating basket along the river bank and found by Pharaoh's daughter who raised him as her son. During a phase in Moses' adulthood, he denounced all familial ties with Pharaoh's daughter and their kingdom and chose to identify with the Israelites who were enslaved and forced to work under harsh conditions. In his heart, Moses knew that God had a greater purpose for his life and it did not consist of him remaining as a privileged grandson of a ruling Pharaoh. I believe Moses viewed the divine purpose of God as being greater than the temporary wealthy, extravagant and pleasurable life Egypt offered. *"By faith Moses, when he was come to years, refused to be called the son of Pharaoh's daughter; Choosing rather to suffer affliction with the people of God, than to enjoy the pleasures of sin for a season"* (Hebrews 11:24, 25). One day while in Egypt, Moses observed an Egyptian beating an Israelite slave. Moses killed the Egyptian and hid the body in the sand. The following day, Moses observed two Israelites at odds with each other. He intervened thinking that both would understand that God would perhaps use him to deliver them from their bondage. When Moses intervened, one of them revealed his killing of an Egyptian and hiding the body the day previous. Moses' killing had also been reported to Pharaoh who sought to apprehend and kill Moses. Murdering an Egyptian was punishable by death. In fear, Moses left Egypt and settled in the land of Midian where he spent forty years as a husband, father, son-in-law, and shepherd.

Moses' time in Midian served as a wilderness season. It was during this phase of his life, while performing shepherding duties that he would have the burning bush experience. God spoke to Moses saying, *"Come now therefore, and I will send thee unto Pharaoh, that thou mayest bring forth my people the children of Israel out of Egypt"* (Exodus 3:10). When the call of God rests on your life, you cannot run from God's beckoning. God is sovereign and He will find you. God was letting Moses know that it was time for him to focus on fulfilling his divine purpose. Through the burning bush experience, Moses was brought to the realization that the yearning he had in his heart to be used by God as a deliverer for God's people, was indeed from God. Moses had finally become acquainted with his divine purpose. God made it clear to Moses that he was called to approach the ruling Pharaoh and demand the release of God's people so that they may journey to the wilderness to worship Him. This would be quite the challenge for Moses as Pharaoh had no intentions of freeing the Israelites from slavery. But, after God inflicted ten plagues on the Egyptians with the last plague being the death of all firstborn Egyptian males, including Pharaoh's son, Pharaoh freed the Israelites and ordered them to leave Egypt. The plagues on the Egyptians proved that God was on the side of the oppressed and he wanted their deliverance for His glory. Their deliverance bears the testimony that God is faithful to his promise and in his timing God will accomplish the word he has decreed or spoken.

Wilderness Seasons Unveil Hidden Heart Issues

Wilderness seasons can be demanding as hidden heart issues are unveiled and brought to the surface. Once the issues surface, it becomes our responsibility to overcome and continue pressing forward in God. Moses' hidden heart issues were unveiled just prior to and during his term of leadership over the nation of Israel. One hidden heart issue that was unveiled in the life of Moses was his failure to submit to the command of God. Failure to submit to the command or word of God angers God and calls for his immediate correction so that we are in alignment with his divine plan. Shortly after Moses and his family left Midian to travel to Egypt, he was given the commandment of circumcision. Moses was to ensure that his son was circumcised. The covenant of circumcision was established by God with Abraham who circumcised his sons and every male living in his household and God wanted it to continue with the nation of Israel, starting with the son of Moses. But, Moses did not circumcise his son as he was instructed. Scripture tells us that during the night, the Lord came to take Moses' life. His wife Zipporah circumcised the son and tossed the sharp stone at his feet. She did not want the son circumcised but reluctantly complied. Exodus 4:25, 26 tells us, *"Then Zipporah took a sharp stone, and cut off the foreskin of her son,*

and cast it at his feet, and said, Surely a bloody husband art thou to me.
So he let him go: then she said, A bloody husband thou art, because of the
circumcision." Moses' failure to submit to God's covenant of
circumcision almost resulted in his death. It displeases the heart
of God when his servants do not act upon his word. God does
not allow us to get away with it. We will bear a consequence.
When God establishes a covenant in the earth, he expects for it
to be adhered to by his people. He does not want us to forfeit
following his word to please someone else or place our desires
over his covenant.

Moses' failure to submit to the command of God was
unveiled another time. In Numbers chapter 20, we see that the
nation of Israel grumbled, complained and quarreled with
Moses about not having water. They faulted Moses for not
having water to drink. They argued that Moses brought them,
their families and livestock to the wilderness region to die.
Egypt, the place of bondage, seemed to be better for them.
Interestingly, as when they were in Egypt, they groaned to God
asking for deliverance from slavery and oppression. Now that
they were delivered, they were complaining. Instead of praying
and seeking God for an answer, they turned to Moses. The
nation of Israel became solely dependent on Moses to seek God
on their behalf and petition Him for their every need. As with
the rigors of leadership, I'm sure Moses having to deal with the
demands of the people was no easy task. He had to manage his
emotions and even frustration with the people. Such a
predicament can be challenging for any leader but God
demands that we honor him. God does not want us to
compromise. Honoring God is to take precedence over the
reactions and thoughts of people.

Moses went before the Lord on the people's behalf and the glory of the Lord appeared. The Lord gave Moses specific instructions concerning how to obtain water. He told Moses to speak to the rock in the presence of the nation of Israel and water would come from the rock. Instead, Moses in his anger against the people, called them 'rebels', hit the rock twice and the water came gushing out. The nation of Israel and their livestock enjoyed the water. However, God dealt with Moses about his disobedience to his spoken word. God is holy and perfect. He wants complete perfection and will confront us when we act contrary to his spoken word or direct command. God chastens and brings correction to those he loves. Moses was loved of God and walked closely with him. But, Moses' closeness with the Lord did not exempt him from correction. Proverbs 3:11, 12 reads, *"My son, despise not the chastening of the Lord; neither be weary of his correction: For whom the Lord loveth he correcteth; even as a father the son in whom he delighteth."* I would prefer God's love and chastening over being isolated and separated from him. I believe in this scenario, Moses became so overwhelmed with the situation at hand and the cry of the people, that he allowed his emotions to supersede God's command. In his anger, he acted contrary to God's instructions. The word of the God tells us to, *"Be ye angry, and sin not: let not the sun go down upon your wrath: Neither give place to the devil"* (Ephesians 4:26, 27). Anger is a healthy emotion. We become angered at some of the behaviors we observe and the negative attitude of others. This is truthful especially with leaders. Leaders are exposed to the good, bad, and the ugly of others. When a leader has a vision, and sees that his or her followers have not yet matured to understand and cooperate with the vision, this can be very disheartening. But, in all instances, we should not allow our anger to control how we respond. Unfortunately, Moses' failure to obey God's word in the presence of the nation of Israel caused for him to miss the blessing of entering the Promised Land. In Numbers 20:12, the Lord says *"...Because ye believed me not, to sanctify me in the eyes of the children of Israel, therefore ye shall not bring this congregation into the land which I have given them."*

During segments of Israel's wilderness experience, Moses became disheartened at their behavior, spiritual dullness, unbelief and rebellion. From the life and leadership experience of Moses, we learn that wilderness seasons require much caution and discipline on the part of leaders as well as followers. Wilderness seasons reveal the imperfections that are stored in the crevices of the heart. Once these imperfections are brought to light, it is our responsibility to approach the Lord in prayer, repent of the wrongdoing, commit to change the behavior and progressively move forward in the fulfillment of our divine purpose.

Wilderness Seasons Enhance the Understanding of Your Role and Responsibility in God's Divine Plan

It is important to understand the role and responsibility God has given in the fulfillment of His divine plan. Otherwise, we operate outside of his plan and create a mess. In examining the life of John the Baptist, I believe the wilderness season he experienced prior to his public ministry, provided clarity and understanding of his role and responsibility in God's divine plan. Before his birth, John's divine purpose was revealed to his father Zacharias by an angel. The angel of the Lord declared to Zacharias, *"For he shall be great in the sight of the Lord, and shall drink neither wine nor strong drink; and he shall be filled with the Holy Ghost, even from his mother's womb. And many of the children of Israel shall he turn to the Lord their God. And he shall go before him in the spirit and power of Elias, to turn the hearts of the fathers to the children, and the disobedient to the wisdom of the just; to make ready a people prepared for the Lord"* (Luke 1: 15 – 17). Following John's birth, those who surrounded his parents were astonished when both agreed to name him John instead of taking his father's name as tradition would dictate. They wondered what John would become as it was evident that the Lord's grace was upon his life.

Concerning John, the Word says, *"And the child grew, and waxed strong in spirit...."* (Luke 1:80). His spiritual growth and development began early. His father, Zacharias being a priest knew the relevance of offering prayer and sacrifices to the Lord. Perhaps, Zacharias taught John the same. Ultimately, we know that it was the Spirit of God that directed and guided John to pursue God's divine purpose. I can attest that it is important to teach and admonish your children in the way of the Lord when they are young. When you are engaged in your children's spiritual lives, equally concerned with their physical as well as spiritual development, and take steps to teach and train them in a manner that propels them to fulfill their divine purpose, they are positioned to seek God concerning their role and responsibility in God's divine plan. When they begin to operate within their role and assume their God given responsibility, the kingdom of God is furthered and your child lives a well-accomplished life.

When examining the life of John, we see that at the time appointed, John went to live in a wilderness region to endure a wilderness season until his ministry was made public. His ministry emerged near the time of Jesus' earthly ministry. There are a few considerations to be made about John's role and responsibility in the kingdom of God that he learned during his wilderness season. First, John understood and made it known to Israel that his role was to be a forerunner of Jesus Christ. As a forerunner, his responsibility entailed declaring the message of repentance, which required that adherents' actions and character demonstrate their conversion. He knew he wasn't the Messiah. He never made any claim to be the Messiah. He acknowledged that his role was to preach the message of righteousness and direct people to Jesus. He did not try or attempt to fill Jesus' shoes in ministry. He remained faithful to his assigned role and managed his responsibility as a bold preacher of repentance while living in the wilderness. John says, *"I indeed baptize you with water; but one mightier than I cometh, the latchet of whose shoes I am not worthy to unloose: he shall baptized you with the Holy Ghost and with fire"* (Luke 3:16). John also says *"He must increase, but I must decrease. He that cometh from above is above all"* (John 3:30,31a). What we learn from the ministry of John is that operating within your divine role eliminates useless efforts as these will only be to your detriment and not your reward. When you operate within your divine role, you are giving God an opportunity to establish dominion in your life.

Second, from John's wilderness season he came to the understanding that he was responsible for promoting the kingdom of God. John did not give-in to suggestions that intended to bring division to the kingdom of God nor did he envision being in competition with Jesus during the time of his ministry. For instance, when John's disciples told him that many were going to Jesus to be baptized, John responded by giving testimony that Jesus is the Christ and he was sent to bear witness of Him. John says, *"Ye yourselves bear me witness, that I said, I am not the Christ, but that I am sent before him"* (John 3:28). John's response to his disciples shows that he understood the need to submit to the ministry of Jesus.

You may be wondering, what do I do if my purpose was not revealed before my birth as John the Baptist? Or, what do I do if my role and responsibility has not been made so clear to me during a wilderness season? Wilderness seasons are the perfect opportunity to spend additional time in prayer asking the Lord to reveal your role and responsibility in his kingdom. Consult God as He is the giver of your role and responsibility. Also, completing a spiritual gifts assessment can be helpful. Assessments are a practical approach to discovering you and your divine role. There are several assessments available online at no cost and I don't recommend one over the other. Assessments identify areas of strengths and of particular interest. Spiritual gifts assessments bring to light aspects of our personality that are oftentimes overlooked but can be of value to the body of Christ. Prayerfully consider the results of your assessment and pray to God for clarity.

Wilderness Seasons Can Bring a Passion for God's Presence

Wilderness seasons can bring a passion for the presence of God. Passion is an intense desire that materializes into a relentless pursuit of drawing closer to God. We should have a

passion for God's presence in our lives. Psalms 16:11 says
..."*In thy presence there is fullness of joy; at thy right hand there are pleasures for evermore.*" There is joy and peace in God's presence that cannot be replaced by natural means. The desire divinely placed in our heart for God is satisfied when we are in his presence. His presence brings complete satisfaction. Our passion for the presence of God in our lives is contagious. It can result in others evaluating their level of commitment and dedication to the Lord. It can lead to others wanting the presence of God in their lives and seek God concerning the fulfillment of their divine purpose.

David expressed his passion for God's presence in Psalms 63. Psalms 63 was penned while David was undergoing a wilderness season. He was fleeing from King Saul who sought to take his life. Saul became jealous and bitterly angry with David after the people of Israel began to attribute admiration and accolades to David following his miraculous defeat of the giant Goliath. Saul turned his demonic fury on David. David was banished from ordinary life and dwelled in the wilderness of Judah. In spite of his life-threatening circumstances, David's passion for God's presence did not die. David was determined to pursue God by drawing closer to Him through prayer, praise, meditation, and memories of God's past extraordinary acts. David says, "*O God, thou art my God; early will I seek thee: my soul thirsteth for thee, my flesh longeth for thee, in a dry and thirsty land where no water is*" (Psalms 63:1). From a logical standpoint, David should have been developing a strategy to stay clear of Saul at the start of his morning, but as noted in verse 1, David's heart was set on pursuing God in the early morning hours of his day. The thirst and longing in his heart for God could only be satisfied when he got into the presence

of the Lord. It is awesome to be in the presen
His presence is filling. In verse 2, David reflects
of the presence of the Lord that he experienced
sanctuary. In Old Testament times, the sanctuary ... the place
of God's presence. God's glory was displayed in the sanctuary.
In verse 3, David tells of the greatness of God's love. He
describes God's love as better than life. He glorifies God
because of his great love. David reaffirms his devotion to the
Lord by declaring in verse 4 that he would praise God and lift
his name or hold his name in high degree for the rest of his life.
David goes on to further say in verse 8, *"My soul followeth hard
after thee: thy right hand upholdeth me"* (Psalms 63:8). David was
expressing his intense desire to seek the Lord and be in His
presence. David understood that it was the Lord who sustained
and protected him from Saul's sentence of death. He
acknowledged the Lord as his protecting force. When our
passion for God's presence is greater than the ordeal we are
undergoing during a wilderness season, we just as David will
experience the joy of heaven here on earth.

Wilderness Seasons Help to Develop Greater Trust in God

Wilderness seasons entail periods of uncertainty and
unexpected events. The biblical character Job experienced a
trying wilderness season. His life was once free of opposition
and troubles but there came a time when he experienced a
deluged of unexpected events marked by periods of uncertainty.
In all that Job encountered, he developed greater trust in God.

Job was characterized as an upright and righteous man. He lived in the land of Uz and was blessed to accumulate much wealth and material possessions. Job was a premiere man of the East, an icon in his region, a distinction that others in his day may have coveted. But, Job experienced a period of intense trials. During his period of intense trials, he learned the importance of developing a greater trust in God. Job's first intense trial involved the loss of his cattle and livestock, the burning of his sheep and the killing of his servants. And, while the person advised him of the first calamity, another delivered news of a second calamity which involved the death of all his children. I can only imagine Job's initial reaction as he heard the news. I'm sure it was overwhelming. The trials of Job were multiplied within a short period of time. He even lost his wealth. But, Job continued in his dedication to the Lord. Job did not have the bible knowledge or availability of scripture text as we have on-hand for our use today. However, Job understood the need to trust God amidst intense trials. In spite of his circumstances, he did not sin or blame God.

Job even experienced sickness and pain (see Job 2:7, 8). During Job's time of sickness and pain, his wife advised him to curse God and die. His wife saw no need to continue trusting God in the midst of his calamity. Yet, Job the righteous man he was, maintained his trust in God and did not sin. When three of Job's friends heard of his calamities and agreed to visit to provide comfort and sympathy, they sat in silence for seven days mourning his sickness and pain. His friends were astonished at the site of Job and how the sickness dominated his physical body, negatively impacting his health and well-being. Afterwards, they each begin to give their reasons for Job's sickness and calamities. They claimed that it must have

been something Job did to cause such grief an
occur. His friends held to the view that Job mu
and caused God to look unfavorable on him. T
was not the case. There was a time in which Job expressed
frustration and disappointment with his life circumstances when
he cursed the day he was born. Job says, *"Let the day perish
wherein I was born, and the night in which it was said, There is a man
child conceived. Let that day be darkness; let not God regard it from
above, neither let the light shine upon it"* (Job 3:3,4). In spite of all the
trials and obstacles, the ungodly advice of his wife and the
erroneous claims made by his friends for his suffering, one truth
is evident; Job developed a greater trust in God. He did not
give-up on God. He did not bring an accusation or charge
against God for his calamities and sickness. And, when his
season of trials and obstacles ended and he prayed for his
friends, God rewarded him double for his trust, endurance and
obedience (see Job 42:10,12-13). What we learn from the
experience of Job is that part of trusting God entails
conditioning our hearts to believe God in spite of unfavorable
life circumstances. Conditioning one's heart is just as important
as physical activity is to the human body. If the body is not
conditioned to engage in physical activity, it will become weak,
fragile, and susceptible to sickness. Medical experts recommend
thirty minutes per day of physical exercise coupled with a
healthy diet for good health. Similarly, our heart must be
conditioned so that no matter the severity of the trial, we
remain true to the Lord and not give-up. An unconditioned
heart is weak, susceptible to unbelief and blinded to the need to
exercise faith.

When we read about Job's challenges and the blessings
of God being multiplied double of what he initially owned and

ossessed, we are reading the account afterwards. The book of Job was not written and given to Job prior to his wilderness season. He was not provided a script, guide or aid that detailed all of what would happen during and after his period of intense trials. Job had to learn the importance of trusting God and patiently wait on God to provide an answer to his solemn requests. The enemy proposed to God that if Job lost his wealth, family, possessions and even health that he would abandon his trust in him. But, this did not happen. Job did not abandon his trust in God.

The experiences of Job demonstrate that during wilderness seasons, God is working behind the scenes on our behalf and he has pre-ordained the blessings we will receive after we have fulfilled his divine plan. We, just as Job, must trust God. When we trust God, we are blessed. When we operate in unbelief and a lack of faith, we miss the blessings God intended and remain in a wilderness season much longer than divinely purposed.

Key Principles

1. Wilderness seasons are designed to prepare us for the fulfillment of our divine purpose.

2. Wilderness seasons require the development of unwavering faith before the manifestation of God's promise.

3. Wilderness seasons demand isolation and separation prior to the release of God's greater blessings.

4. When we cooperate with God, the duration of our wilderness season is in accordance with God's divine plan.

Prayer

Lord, I commit to center my life on the truth of your word and I will trust you with all of my heart. May I learn the lessons you have purposed during my wilderness season, in Jesus' name, Amen.

Study Questions for Chapter Five are on page 158

Chapter Six

Prayer and Intimacy
with the Lord

One thing have I desired of the Lord, that will I seek after; that I may dwell in the house of the Lord all the days of my life, to behold the beauty of the Lord, and to inquire in his temple.

Psalms 27:4

What is Prayer?

A divine purposed life can only be accomplished through sincere devotion to prayer. Prayer serves as the foundation of our relationship with Christ. Prayer gives us access to the heavenlies. We can tap into God's unlimited supply of spiritual resources through prayer. Prayer takes on varying definitions. One of the simplest and commonly accepted definitions of prayer is communication and one-on-one contact with the Lord. There are numerous examples in scripture of this definition, one being exampled in the life of Hannah who prayed earnestly to the Lord requesting a child. In her communication and one-on-one contact with the Lord, Hannah poured out her soul. She wept as she expressed her sincere and earnest desire to conceive a child. *"And she was in bitterness of soul, and prayed unto the Lord, and wept sore. And she vowed a vow, and said, O Lord of hosts, if thou wilt indeed look on the affliction of thine handmaid, and remember me, and not forget thine handmaid, but wilt give unto thine handmaid a man child, then I will give him unto the Lord all the days of his life, and there shall no rasor come upon his head"* (I Samuel 1:10, 11). Hannah did not fear or doubt that God would not grant her request for a son. So, in God's appointed season, Hannah conceived and gave birth to the prophet Samuel who was dedicated to the Lord in accordance with the Mosaic law and lived in the temple all the days of his life. Samuel became a mighty prophet in Israel.

When we examine the actions of Hannah in prayer, we see that when she pours out her soul before the Lord, she approaches God in faith. Faith is required when approaching God. *"But without faith it is impossible to please him: for he that cometh to God must believe that he is, and the he is a rewarder of them that diligently seek him"* (Hebrews 11:6). In Hannah's request to the Lord, she did not seek the blessing of a male child to satisfy her longing or for selfish motives but to give that child in service to the Lord. When we submit our requests before the Lord, we should see if the request is one that will please God or seek to advance His kingdom. If our requests are based on selfish motives, God will not grant our requests.

Prayer can also be defined as a commitment to be in the presence of the Lord. It entails a decision on the part of the believer to commit to its practice daily and sacrifice the time necessary to develop a lifestyle of being in the presence of the Lord. Jesus says, *"... Men [women] ought always to pray, and not to faint"* (Luke 18:1). The key to remaining in the presence of the Lord is a consistent life of prayer. Fainters are those who lose sight of God's presence and they become victims of their own error. When we commit to pray, we are empowering the angelic host of heaven to minister on our behalf and assist in bringing about God's purposes in the earth. This is why prayer is so important. Heaven moves when we extend the invitation through prayer. God intervenes when we ask of Him to do so in prayer. Prayer is the essence of our spiritual life. Just as breathing is vital to sustain physical life, prayer is vital to sustain our spiritual life in Christ. Our divine purpose will not be fulfilled if we lack a commitment to prayer. Prayer must be a main priority.

I recall reading the inspiring life account of a woman who devoted her life to prayer. She prayed for her husband, the ministry they were entrusted and of course other needs. As time progressed, their local ministry grew and her prayer ministry expanded throughout the United States. Testimonies across denominational lines came by the thousands of people who were healed of various ailments and lifelong sicknesses as a result of her prayers. What I find noteworthy about her life is that she had such a deep love for the presence of God that prayer was as natural to her as breathing. Prayer was not a routine or religious exercise that she practiced only during a period of life struggles. She lived a life of prayer. Prayer was of such great importance that she structured her life around it. She did not allow anyone or anything to interfere with her devotion to prayer. When you know what God has purposed for you, you should take the initative to structure your life around it. When you make such a decision, you are allowing the purpose God has established for you to be a top priority.

One noted example in scripture of one who committed to remain in the presence of the Lord, is the prophetess Anna. Anna was a widow of the lineage of Phanuel. After her husband's death, she dedicated her life to prayer and lived in the temple. New Testament scripture points out that the prophetess Anna served God with fastings and prayers day and night. Anna greatly valued being in the presence of the Lord. As a result of her devotion to prayer, she was blessed to see Jesus Christ, Israel's redeemer, as an infant. She was given the opportunity to see the fullfillment of the prophecies declared thousands of years before that a redeemer would come to save his people from their sins.

I am reminded of the legacy of my dearest mother-in-law. She was a woman of prayer. Prior to meeting her in-person, my husband, who I was dating at the time, showed a photograph of her to me. I remember seeing a purity in her eyes that transcended human comprehension as I looked at the photograph. I commented to him that she was a woman that displayed great internal and external beauty. It was then that he began to reveal to me that his mother was a woman of prayer. He advised that she consistently went before the Lord in prayer. Prayer was interwoven into her daily life. She prayed for her children and petitioned God for the needs of her family. My mother-in-law was a woman of amazing faith. She was widowed in her early forties. She assumed the responsibility of rearing thirteen children, eleven of which were boys, as a result of her husband's death. This would be a test of faith that some would not imagine experiencing. But, her prayers gave her the courage to take on the responsibility of child rearing and to do it with such love, care and amazing grace. She skillfully managed the affairs of her home and displayed the character of Christ so that her children would see the value of living for God and being good stewards in his kingdom. I had the opportunity of sharing a hotel room with her once while vacationing in one of the southern states. At the beginning of the day, she was on her knees praying to the Lord and at the end of the day, once again she was on her knees spending time in the presence of the Lord. I admired her devotion and diligence to prayer. There are blessings that my family and I are experiencing today because of her devotion to prayer. At her homegoing service, the testimony that all of her children were Christ followers was the zenith of all accolades. A consistent life of prayer contributed to her success.

Two Commonly Practiced Prayers

There are several types of prayers but two of the most commonly practiced prayers are intercessory and prayers of petitions and requests. Intercessory prayer is the act of representing the best interest, need or desire of one or more persons to God. Intercessory prayer involves expressing a God-birthed desire related to the spiritual well-being of another to the Lord. Intercession requires that the intercessor yield to the leading of the Holy Spirit at anytime on behalf of another. An intercessor is one who is committed to presenting the needs of others to the Lord. An intercessor meets the Lord in prayer on behalf of another requesting his divine intervention. As an intercessor, I can attest to being awakened at various hours of the night and called upon at unpredictable times of the day to intercede for one or more persons. In some cases, the Lord will make it clear concerning the need of an individual(s) or groups you are interceding on behalf of. In some cases, it may not be made clear concerning the need but I've learned that my responsibility as an intercessor is to pray and allow God to orchestrate and workout the details.

As believers, we have been called by God to intercede on behalf of others. When we answer the call of God to intercede for others, we are operating within our divine purpose. We are to intercede on behalf of our family and friends and those within our circle of influence. We are to intercede for humanity and government rulers and authorities. I Timothy 2:1,2 says, *"I exhort therefore that, first of all, supplications, prayers, intercessions, and giving of thanks, be made for all men; For kings, and for all that are in authority; that we may lead a quiet and peaceable life in all godliness and honesty."* We are to intercede for the body of Christ. Ephesians 6:18 says, *"Praying always with all prayer and supplication in the Spirit, and watching thereunto with all perseverance and supplication for all saints."* The body of Christ is comprised of saints of God. We are to intercede for the nation of Israel. Psalms 122:6 says,

"Pray for the peace of Jerusalem: they shall prosper that love thee." We should intercede for the salvation of the nation of Israel. The Apostle Paul says concerning the salvation of the nation of Israel, *"Brethern, my heart's desire and prayer to God for Israel is, that they might be saved"* (Romans 10:1). The desire for Israel's salvation was God-birthed and Paul dedicated himself to intercession on their behalf. Interestingly, as today, more and more Jews are hearing the gospel and coming to faith in Christ Jesus. Our intercession for Israel should be the same as the Apostle Paul, that they be saved by coming to faith in Christ Jesus. As we offer prayers of intercession on behalf of the aforementioned, we are giving God the opportunity to bring about his projected purposes in their lives and in the case of government leaders, our prayers of intercession are that the region of their rulership will contribute to the expansion of God's kingdom in the earth.

Prayers of petitions and requests are probably the most commonly prayed in Christendom. These are prayers that involve the believer coming before the Lord and asking God to act, respond, or judge in a manner that brings heaven's blessings to earth. Generally, these prayers involve the believer praying for the manifestation of a need or desire. Prayers of petitions and requests require approaching God in confidence. I John 5:14, 15 says, *"And this is the confidence that we have in him, that, if we ask any thing according to his will, he heareth us; And if we know that he hear us, whatsover we ask, we know that we have the petitions that we desired of him."* When we request, petition or ask in agreement with His divine will, he hears and grants our request. When submitting prayers of petitions and requests to the Lord, the believer should not have any anxiety, stress or worry. These prayers should be followed by praise and thanksgiving.

Philippians 4:6,7 says, *"Be careful for nothing; but in everything by prayer and supplication with thanksgiving let your requests be made known unto God. And the peace of God, which passeth all understanding, shall keep your hearts and minds through Christ Jesus."* God's peace extends beyond human comprehension. His peace provides comfort and ease relieving the tendency to stress or worry.

Benefits of Prayer

Prayer is the best investment of earthly time. It yields blessings that are beneficial here on earth and in heaven. Jesus says, *"Lay not up for yourselves treasures upon earth, where moth and rust doth corrupt, and where thieves break through and steal: But lay up for yourselves treasures in heaven, where neither moth nor rust doth corrupt, and where thieves do not break through nor steal: For where your treasure is, there will your heart be also"* (Matthew 6:19-21). You are storing treasures in heaven when you invest time in prayer. I can recall the testimony of my paternal grandmother. She was a woman of prayer and monetary giving. She could be often seen placing her name on envelopes and giving to various ministries that worked to advance the kingdom of God in the earth. This is one spiritual legacy my grandmother left for our family. My grandmother passed away at the age of one-hundred and one while sleeping. However, a few years ago, by way of a dream, the Lord allowed me to see my grandmother in heaven and I noticed that she had a large treasure box filled with precious gems. She was so pleased with her treasure box that she began grabbing and placing several gems around her neck. The Lord revealed to me that the treasure box my grandmother received was as a result of her diligence to prayer and her relentless sacrifical giving to the kingdom of God. At the moment the

Lord revealed this truth to me concerning my grandmother, I gained a deeper understanding concerning the value of prayer and monetary giving. Both prayer and giving are important to God. God rewards us richly not only in our present life but also in heaven when we diligently do both.

Prayer helps to maintain proper balance so that you wisely and skillfully manage the complexities of daily life. Daily life can be complex when you consider the multiple responsibilities, layers of commitment, and obligations. I consider my role as a wife, mother, ministry leader, and professional career woman as varied and layered with multiple duties and responsibilities. I've found that at the start of my day, when I make the commitment to spend time in prayer with the Lord, the remainder of my day is far more productive. Each time you make the sacrifice to spend time with the Lord in prayer, at the start of your day, you are training your mind to place the purposes of God at the center of your day. Also, you are focused on prioritizing so that God receives the maximum benefit from what is accomplished. This helps you to develop the much needed discipline to focus on tasks, assignments, and responsibilities that contribute to the fulfillment of your divine purpose.

The prophet Daniel wisely and skillfully managed daily life. He was committed to the purposes of God and placed a high priority on spending time with the Lord while performing his civic duties in the Babylonian kingdom. Daniel, along with a few other men of Judah, were selected to be a part of the Babylonian king's special counsel due to their special intelligence, knowledge and understanding. He served as an advisor to the king, the equivalent to a presidential cabinet member in the democratic government of our nation. His life was interrupted by the Babylonian and Persian invasion of Jerusalem. The people of God, in particular, the tribe of Judah, was taken captive by the Babylonians and forced to serve under their rulership. Judah's captivity was due to their disobedience and unfaithfulness to God. Disobedience and unfaithfulness was a constant theme throughout the history of God's covenant people. Although taken captive, Daniel did not become laxed in his spirituality. He was well disciplined in his approach to spiritual matters and remained dedicated to the Lord. Three times daily, Daniel faithfully prayed to the Lord and spent time in the Lord's presence. As a result of his faithfulness to prayer, God entrusted heavenly mysteries to him.

Prayer provides an avenue for us to experience the joy of fellowship with God. It satisfies the deep longing of our heart and temporarily quenches the thirst we have for eternity. As believers, we have a deep longing for eternity and being in our eternal home. While our primary focus is to fulfull the will of God in the generation we've been called to serve, we also want to experience the joy of fellowship with God. Fellowship brings us closer to God and deepens our connection with heaven, our eternal habitat. Prayer provides a means for us to enjoy eternity while living in the present. As we continually make contact with God through prayer, our spiritual senses are developed and sharpened.

The glory or visible presence of the Lord that displays His splendor and radiance is manifested as a result of a life of consistent prayer. When we consistently pray, the Lord rewards us openly by manifesting his glory. In the Old Testatment, the glory of the Lord was manifested to the Israelites as a pillar of cloud by day and fire by night. This visible sign of God's presence followed them throughout their wilderness journey. *"And the Lord went before them by day in a pillar of a cloud, to lead them the way; and by night in a pillar of fire, to give them light; to go by day and night: He took not away the pillar of cloud by day, nor the pillar of fire by night, from before the people"* (Exodus 13:21, 22). This visible presence of God served as a constant reminder of his presence dwelling among his people.

During the wilderness journey, Moses spent a great deal of time in the presence of the Lord. Moses was known to spend forty days and forty nights without any food or drink in the presence of the Lord at Mount Sinai (see Exodus 34:28). In one instance, when Moses came down from Mount Sinai, after the Lord gave him the commandments on new tablets of stone, his face was radiant because he had spoken directly with the Lord. Moses was not aware of this radiance until he observed the reaction of his brother Aaron and the Israelites who did not want to come near him because of it. After speaking with Aaron and the Israelites, Moses then placed a veil over his face to cover the radiance that beamed as a result of him being in the glory of the Lord. He made it a practice to remove the veil whenever he was in the presence of the Lord and speaking with Him. But, when he returned among the people, he placed the veil over his face until he returned to the presence of the Lord. I believe as Moses spent time in the presence of the Lord, he began to take on heavenly characteristics. Besides Jesus our Savior, scripture does not reveal any other person who spent the amount of time Moses did in the presence of the Lord. Moses knew the Lord face to face. Deuteronomy 34:10 says, *"And there arose not a prophet since in Israel like unto Moses, whom the Lord know face to face."*

Remember, Moses was under the old covenant. Under the new covenant, God continues to call his people to a higher level of prayer and intimacy but only a small percentage answer the call. Generally, those who answer the call to a higher level of prayer and intimacy may become labeled as "too spiritual" or "fanatical believers". These assigned labels and others of a similar kind should serve as motivation to continue purusing a higher level of closeness with the Lord and fulfill our divine purpose.

God continues to manifest his visible presence amongst his people and it can be seen by others. II Corinthians 3: 7 – 11 tells us that if the old covenant (i.e. the giving of the law) ushered in a radiance such that Aaron and the Israelites could not look at the face of Moses, the new covenant (i.e. salvation by grace through faith in Jesus Christ) brings about a greater glory.

My husband and I attended a conference several years ago and the conference speaker pointed out my husband while ministering. He noted that my husband had a visible display of God's glory on his forehead, describing this display as a glowing dot. During this time period, my husband was spending additional time in prayer. I can recall him coming home from his busy job as an Internet Car Sales Manager and going into his prayer closet for several hours. In some cases, he was in prayer throughout the night. God provided him with the strength to go to work the following day renewed and ready for the task at hand. He continued to do well with sales during his seasons of prayer. But, this additional time in prayer brought about a change in his appearance. I noticed that he had a visible glow that beamed around him. Prior to the speaker ministering a prophetic message to my husband, he pointed out to those assembled that the manifest presence of God was displayed on his forehead and that my husband had been with the Lord. God was visibly manifesting his glory on my husband and this glory is what the conference speaker was seeing and making known to the congregation at the conference.

Hindrances to Prayer

Prayers can be hindered if the heart of the believer is tainted with unforgiveness. Jesus says, *"And when ye stand praying, forgive, if ye have ought against any: that your Father also which is in heaven may forgive you your trespasses"* (Mark 11:25). Our prayers are hindered when we harbor unforgiveness. Unforgiveness formulates and grows in the heart due to unresolved conflict. When a conflict or matter goes without discussion or some form of resolution, the conflict continues to play in the mind. Oftentimes, what gets played in the mind are extremes that are rooted in carnality and if you are not careful, you can easily fall into the deceptive trap of unforgiveness. Unforgiveness is sin and if not repented of it will lead to continual sin. Therefore, it is imperative that conflicts are promptly dealt with and settled so the believer does not fall into this deceptive trap. Forgiveness allows the believer to pray to God with freedom and confidence.

Offenses will come. We will encounter offenses. The word of God brings this spiritual truth to light. Offenses are a part of the believer's journey of faith and we should not allow offenses to deter us from fulfilling our divine purpose. Offenses that occur within and even outside the body of Christ should be dealt with as soon as possible. Of course, when handling an offense with someone who is a part of or outside the body of Christ, we should remain prayerful and depending on the severity of the situation, seek godly counsel concerning the best approach to take to resolve the issue. We must be careful to follow the biblical method when we approach our sister or brother in the Lord concerning an offense. Scripture exhorts us to take a practical, face-to-face approach. St. Matthew 18:15 – 17 says, *"Moreover if thy brother shall trespass against thee, go and tell him his fault between thee and him alone: if he shall hear thee, thou hast gained thy brother. But, if he will not hear thee, then take with thee one or two more, that in the mouth of two or three witnesses every word may be established. And if he shall neglect to hear them, tell it unto the church: but if he neglect to hear the church, let him be unto thee as a heathen man and a publican."*

First, we approach our sister or brother in the Lord with the intent of reconciling the relationship. In this regard, we are not losing our sister or brother to the world. If the first approach is unsuccessful, we are to take one to three believers to assist in the reconciliation process. If the second approach does not resolve the issue, then we are to inform the church body and bring it before them for resolution. And, if the brother or sister refuses to resolve the matter after it has been presented before the church, then they should be considered and treated as an unbeliever. If we are unable to forgive our sister or brother in the Lord of their wrongdoing, then our Heavenly Father will not forgive us. Jesus says, *"For if ye forgive men their trespasses, your heavenly Father will also forgive you: But if ye forgive not men their trespasses, neither will your Father forgive your trespasses"* (Matthew 6: 14, 15). The foundational premise of the Chrisitan faith is forgiveness. We are indebted to forgive others as God has forgiven us of the debt of sin, a debt we could never in our own power, might or strength re-pay.

In the parable of the unforgiving servant, Jesus teaches the necessity of forgiveness and warns against the danger of unforgiveness (see Matthew 18:23 – 35). In this parable, there was a servant who owed his master an insurmountable debt. It was a debt that the servant would never earn enough money to re-pay in his lifetime. The servant's master ordered that the servant, his wife, children, and all that he possessed be sold to repay the debt. The servant begged his master to be patient with him allowing the debt to be re-paid. The master was gracious and loving toward the servant. He forgave the debt and freed him from the obligation. This same servant who was forgiven of his debt, found someone who owed him the equivalent of a few dollars and began demanding that the debt be re-paid. When the person asked the forgiven servant if he would allow him an opportunity to re-pay the debt, he refused and had the person thrown into prison until the debt was re-paid. When the forgiven servant's master heard of his, he sternly rebuked him for his unmerical and unforgiving heart. The master then had the once forgiven servant thrown into prison to be tortured until the debt was re-paid. Jesus teaches that God will treat us as the master treated the once forgiven servant, unless we forgive our sister or brother in the Lord. The flames of hell fire will serve as a witness to an unforgiving heart. God wants us to have a forgiving heart. A forgiving heart serves as a symbol of the indwelling power of the Holy Spirit. It is also a witness to the unsaved community of the forgiving nature of God.

Unrepented sin is a hindrance to prayer. Unrepented sin creates a barrier between the believer and God and the believer's prayers are not heard. The Psalmist declares in Psalms 66:18, *"If I regard iniquity in my heart, the Lord will not hear me."* We are responsible for confessing our sin to the Lord and asking for forgiveness. I John 1:9 says, *"If we confess our sins, he is faithful and just to forgive us our sins, and to cleanse us from all unrigteousness."* One way unrepented sin develops is as a result of bitterness. Bitterness seeks to destroy the cleanliness of the heart. It leaves wounds that penetrate and negatively impact the entire being – spirit, soul, and body. Ephesians 4:31, 32 says, *"Let all bitterness, and wrath, and anger, and clamour, and evil speaking, be put away from you, with all malice. And be ye kind one to another, tenderhearted, forgiving one another, even as God for Christ's sake hath forgiven you."* Research shows a linkage between bitterness, one's quality of life and health. Individuals who harbor bitterness for extended periods of time tend to experience health problems or be afflicted with disease. These individuals are least likely to forgive. The word of God teaches us to, *"Keep thy heart with all diligence; for out of it are the issues of life"* (Proverbs 4:23). This means we are responsible for what is allowed in and out of our hearts. We must make every effort to not allow roots of bitterness to be planted in our hearts. Our hearts are delicate and should be a sanctuary for the presence of the Holy Spirit. The Holy Spirit will not dwell in a place filled with darkness and roots of evil. The Holy Spirit seeks to live in a place of peace, purity and love. A heart of bitterness contains no elements of these virtues.

I remember sharing with a colleague an incident that ocurred within my immediate family. This incident led to bad feelings and an unwillingness from one of the parties to settle the issue. During the time period of silence, the other party earnestly sought the Lord. She was uncertain of how to approach the relative after making a few failed attempts. After a few months of attempting to resolve the issue, the once unwilling party finally agreed to speak about the matter and independently contacted the family member. It was an answer to prayer. During the phone discussion, both settled the matter and began developing a good relationship. My colleague commented that the manner in which a Christian resolves an issue is completely different than what she was accustomed as she was from a non-Christian background. She was amazed at how the issue was resolved and the effort both made to develop a healthy relationship.

A divided home is another hindrance to prayer. A divided home lacks stability and the peace of God. In a divided home, the husband and the wife have their own agenda. Instead of working together to fulfuill the purposes of God, each act as independent agents bringing confusion and in some cases strife in the home. It is important for the husband and wife to surrender their will to the Lord. When one enters marriage, both become one in flesh. Genesis 2:24 says, *"Therefore shall a man leave his father and his mother, and shall cleave unto his wife: and they shall be one flesh."* Spiritually, the two becoming one happens at the instant both are joined together in marriage. This spiritual bond becomes a greater reality daily as both continually grow in grace and the intimate knowledge of God's divine purpose. Husbands are encouraged to be considerate of their wives, treating them with respect and as heirs of the gift of salvation. Behavior contrary to this encouragement hinders the prayers of the husband, and for that matter, even the wife if she also behaves in the same manner. I Peter 3:7 says, *"Likewise, ye husbands, dwell with them according to knowledge, giving honor unto the wife, as unto the weaker vessel, and as being heirs together of the grace of life; that your prayers be not hindered."* Love, honor, and respect are the bedrock of a good marital relationship. If either is non-existent, the marriage will be tumultous and the home an unbearable place to dwell. The home of married believers should be a place of peace and welcoming to those who need prayer, upliftment and deliverance.

Intimacy with the Lord

A consistent life of prayer helps to formulate a close and intimate bond with the Lord. Intimacy with the Lord is key to fulfilling your divine purpose. Intimacy is developed as we continually pursue the heart of the Lord. The Lord desires to know us more closely and this must be our desire when pursuing him. The Psalmist David is known as a man after God's own heart. *"... I have found David the son of Jesse, a man after my own heart, which shall fulfill my will"* (Acts 13:22). This means David was one who pursued God with great passion and fervor. His love for God was greater than his love for his position as king, material possessions, and wealth. He geninuely loved God. It is not coincidental that David is the writer of many of the psalms that we are encouraged by today. When these psalms are sung or played on instruments, we experience the grand presence of God. Intimacy with the Lord is to be valued. It should be the primary reason we passionately pursue God.

When Jesus appointed his disciples to ministry, he called them to first be with him followed by sending them forth to preach the gospel of the kingdom. Interesting that the first calling given to the disciples was closeness with Jesus. Mark

3:13, 14 says, *"And he [Jesus] goeth up into a mountain, and calleth unto him whom he would: and they came unto him. And he ordained twelve, that they should be with him, and that he might send them forth to preach."* Notice that Jesus called those who he wanted and they came to him. Jesus desired more than anything that his disciples first know and become acquainted with him. This tells us that the invitation to intimacy is extended by our Lord and it is our responsibility to receive and act on the invitation. Intimacy with the Lord is a continual quest that is to be valued throughout the journey of the believer. We place ourselves in a position to know the plans the Lord has ordained for our lives through intimacy.

The Resemblance Effect

The more time we spend cultivating a close and intimate bond with the Lord, we begin to take on his nature and character. We begin to resemble our Lord in many fashions and godly qualities become integrated into our inward being. Our will and motivation become aligned with his purposes. Heavenly deposits are made into our inward being and we are changed into the glorious image of our Lord. The process of our resemblance mirrors our earthly family. Children resemble their parents in physical appearance and natural characteristics. DNA dictates much of the physical appearance and characteristics. The more time the parent and child spend together developing their relationship, the child takes on more of the parent's natural characteristics. Looking at our children, my youngest daughter resembles me and my husband. I noticed that my eldest daughter resembles me and has taken on some of my natural characteristics. At times, she likes to wear my style of clothing, jewelry, and in some instances she replicates my speech. My son resembles my husband in physical appearance and tends to take on the natural characteristics of his father. He likes books, reading, and helping others. I find great joy in watching my son put forth an effort in helping someone feel welcomed in our home. We are a part of God's family and the more contact we make with heaven, the more heavenly characteristics we take on. The more time we spend drawing closer to the Lord, the more we resemble him. Heaven's DNA is deposited into our spirit being and we are conformed to the likeness of Jesus Christ.

The eleven early church apostles spent a great deal of time with Jesus during his earthly ministry. After Jesus' death and resurrection and the in-filling of the Holy Spirit at Pentecost, the early church apostles did mighty acts to advance the kingdom of God. In their efforts to spread the message of truth throughout the city of Jerusalem, they encountered a man who had been unable to walk since birth. This lame man sat by the temple gate asking for monetary assistance daily. When Peter and John encountered this man, they commanded in the name of Jesus that he be healed. Instantly, this man who had been crippled since birth and was probably an icon in this community was healed. This healing miracle prompted the people of Jerusalem to listen attentively to the message of Peter. Peter boldly proclaimed the power and resurrection of Jesus Christ and more than five-thousand people were saved. The religious leaders of Israel had Peter and John jailed and later brought in for questioning. When the leaders observed the boldness and courage of Peter and John, they noted one main characteristic: *they had been with Jesus.* They recognized the authority, power, and boldness of their speech. They knew that these men had been influenced, mentored, trained, discipled and closely acquainted with Jesus. It was undeniable. Their zeal and determination mirrored that of Jesus. Jesus had greatly influenced and transformed their lives to such a degree that it was recognized by the religious and political adversaries who sought to destroy and bring an utter end to their ministry.

Distractions to Intimacy with the Lord

Distractions serve to deter us from making steps towards the accomplishment of our divine purpose. Distractions will prevent us from pursuing intimacy with the Lord. Our valued time can be taken from us when we pursue ventures that are not within the will or plan of God. Distractions are meant to turn our focus from being Christ-centered to indulging in carnality. When the influence of carnal culture becomes greater than the discipline of a spirit-filled life, this is evidence that a distraction is present. Distractions are manifested in varying forms such as unprofitable relationships, busy work, that is, work without a significant purpose, obsession with an object or material possession and the list goes on. Distractions can be presented as appealing and in some cases the right and best action at the time. However, distractions are strategically designed to hinder you from the accomplishment of your divine purpose. It is important to recognize, identify and not become involved with distractions.

During seasons that I set my heart to fast and pray, occasionally I was inundated with phone calls, people wanting to catch-up and check my status. While I certainly did not mind someone briefly conversing with me for the purpose of checking my status, I found that if I did not consciously monitor the amount of time I spent on the phone and put an end to the discussion after a set period of time, the call would go on not giving me much time to diligently pursue God. I found that it worked best for me to designate the amount of time I would spend on phone calls and stick to it. This was not to be anti-social but to ensure that the limited time I was given after coming home from a long day of work was not ruined in lengthy discussions. You have to set limits on your time. The concluding chapter contains tips for effective time management.

Allowing a distraction to take priority over spiritual matters can be quite harmful to the fulfillment of your divine purpose as proven in the life of David. During a period of time in which the spiritual climate dictated that kings go to war, David made the error of remaining in Jerusalem and sending his soldiers out to the battlefield to fight. David's decision to remain within the confines of his dwelling place was one that later cost him greatly. One evening while David took a walk around on the roof of his palace, he noticed a woman named Bathsheba bathing and he commissioned someone in the palace to inquire. David called for this woman and engaged in an adulterous affair as she was married to one of his warriors, Uriah. In his desire to cover-up his sinful act, David had Uriah pulled from the battlefield and brought home, thinking Uriah would be intimate with his wife. But, Uriah had the heart of a warrior. He understood the spiritual climate, followed the requirements of the Mosaic Law and recognized the need to act accordingly. Prior to going to war (see Deuteronomy 20: 5 – 8), the Mosaic law prescribed that if a man built a new house, he must dedicate it; if a man planted a vineyard and did not have the opportunity to eat of its yield, he must allot time to do so; if a man was engaged to be married, he must remain at home; and, if a man was fearful, he must remain at home to prevent fear from spreading throughout the army. Uriah did not meet any of these descriptions. He was qualified, ready, equipped and destined for battle. Uriah, unlike David, was not distracted. He understood that Israel was in a season of war.

Uriah did not allow anything to hinder him from fulfilling his warrior duties. Uriah understood his assignment as a soldier and was dedicated to fighting with the armies of Israel. So, when he returned to David, after being on the battlefield, he refused to go home after being instructed by David to do so. Uriah slept at the entrance of the palace and when David asked the reason, Uriah noted that he could not return home to eat, drink and be with his wife while the ark, Israel and Judah lived in tents, and the armies of Israel engaged in warfare. David made a second attempt to get Uriah to return home; by giving him too much to drink but Uriah did the same. He did not return home. After David recognized that Uriah would not bend on his convictions, David provided Uriah with his death letter. Uriah, the honorable and noble man he was, did not read or open the contents of this letter but followed the instructions of David and provided it to his commander Joab. Uriah died in war and David assumed that his sinful act of adultery had been covered. But, David could not hide his sinful act from God. God sees and knows all things. God used the prophet Nathan to bring to light David's sin and David repented of his wrongdoing. The child that Bathsheba carried as a result of their adulterous affair died. David later married Bathsheba and both had a son named Solomon. What we learn from the experience of David is that a distraction can displease the heart of God and cost us time and wasted effort. This is the reason we should not allow a distraction in our lives.

Key Principles

1. The fulfillment of our divine purpose is connected to the strength of our prayer life.

2. Prayer gives us access to the heavenlies.

3. Prayer allows us to tap into the invisible realm of the spirit and bring heaven's will for our lives into the visible realm.

4. We have heaven's support when we pray according to the will of God.

5. As we are more consistent in prayer, our level of intimacy with the Lord deepens.

6. We should not allow distractions in our lives because they are designed to hinder us from accomplishing our divine purpose.

Prayer

Lord, I ask for divine wisdom to effectively manage my time so that I maintain a consistent life of prayer. As I spend time waiting in your presence, let my love for you grow and my level of intimacy increase in Jesus' name, Amen.

Study Questions for Chapter Six are on pages 159 - 160

Chapter Seven

Spiritual Dreams and Visions

And it shall come to pass in the last days, saith God, I will pour out my Spirit upon all flesh: and your sons and your daughters shall prophesy, and your young men shall see visions, and your old men shall dream dreams.

Acts 2:17

The Significance of Dreams

Dreams consist of a series of pictures, images, or caricatures that are unveiled while one is in a state of sleep. Dreams are common to the human experience. Through dreams, God unveils his divine purposes and gives insight into the past, present and future. Dreams can provide greater understanding concerning major life decisions. Dreams can confirm a message God is speaking. Dreams are important in the life of a believer. Through dreams, we can have supernatural experiences with the Lord.

The old patriarch Jacob had a supernatural experience with the Lord by way of a dream. Jacob dreamt of a stairway that extended from earth to heaven and the angels of the Lord were ascending and descending. The Lord spoke to Jacob during this experience and said, "*I am the Lord God of Abraham thy father, and the God of Isaac: the land whereon thou liest, to thee will I give it, and to thy seed; And thy seed shall be as the dust of the earth, and thou shalt spread abroad to the west, and to the east, and to the north, and to the south: and in thee and in thy seed shall all the families of the earth be blessed*" (Genesis 28:13b, 14). When Jacob awakened, he realized that he had an encounter with the Lord and that the Lord's presence was in the place where he slept. Through this dream, God was reminding Jacob of the promise he made to his father and grandfather concerning their inheritance and the blessing they'd be to future generations. God was letting Jacob know that he was included in this inheritance and blessing to future generations. The place where Jacob rested was a portal, that is a doorway into the heavenlies and the place of God's presence. Jacob renamed the place where he slept "Bethel" meaning the house of God. Jacob knew that from the supernatural experience, the presence of the Lord was in the place where he rested. God chooses to manifest his presence by way of dreams. We must be open to receive the blessing of His presence when He chooses to visit in this manner. We must remember that God desires to create a place of habitation in us through the person of the Holy Spirit. We are to serve as portals of God's presence.

God continues to speak to his people and provide promises by way of dreams, just as He did with the partriarch Jacob. Dreams that are in alignment with God's Word, dreams that confirm a message the Lord relayed by the Holy Spirit, and dreams that provide encouragement and comfort have their origin in God. These are spiritual dreams. We must be alert and attentive to note the dreams that are from God. Dreams that are from God speak messages to us, provide understanding and direction concerning our divine purpose. We must sharpen our understanding of dreams from God so that we can accurately interpret the message God is communicating. Dreams that stem from the natural realm as a result of our daily activities, interactions, or natural processess of the mind are natural dreams. Natural dreams can reveal our own proclivities. Some natural dreams may be of value and can help us identify areas of improvement. Dreams that are from the demonic realm are ungodly and deceptive. Dreams from the demonic realm seek to draw us away from God and fulfilling his purposes. We are to exercise authority over these type of dreams.

Spiritual Dreams Reveal the Condition of the Heart

When examining the life of King Nebuchadnezzar, God used a dream to reveal the condition of his heart. Nebuchadnezzar ruled in the kingdom of Babylon. Babylon was a great and prosperous kingdom. Nebuchadnezzar was a high and lofty leader. He elevated himself above others. His actions were motivated by the desire to accumulate wealth and fortune and rooted in deep seated pride. His heart was impure. God, in his divine love, gave him a dream that showed the condition of his heart (see Daniel 4: 1 - 18). Nebuchadnezzar was fearful and pondered the dream knowing that it was important for it to be interpreted. Initially, he summoned all the magicians, wise men and astrologers in his kingdom to give the interpretation of the dream. However, they were unable to interpret the dream. Daniel went before Nebuchadnezzar who told Daniel the dream and asked him to interpret it. Daniel provided him with the interpretation. He noted that the dream applied to the king. God had issued a decree against him because he had become proud and arrogant. He would be driven away to live with the wild animals and beasts of the field for seven years. He would have the mind of an animal and not a human being. But, his kingdom would be restored when he acknowledged that the God of heaven rules in the kingdom of men. Daniel pleaded and urged the king to renounce his sinfulness, repent, and acknowledge the God of heaven. In doing such, he would prevent such a tragedy and his prosperity would remain. But, Nebuchadnezzar did not listen to Daniel's plea. He did not repent of the pride that was rooted in his heart. Instead of taking the interpretation of the dream seriously and repenting of his pride, he did the opposite. Approximately one year afterwards, the dream as interpreted by

Daniel was fulfilled. He ended up living with the wild animals and beasts of the field for a period of time, experiencing a loss of sanity. After the period of time, and undergoing such a humbling experience, Nebuchadnezzar acknowledged that the God of heaven rules in the kingdom of men (see Daniel 4: 34 – 37). He learned that God's kingdom endures forever. From the experience of Nebuchadnezzar, we see what happens when a person fails to repent of their wrongdoing. When a dream reveals the condition of your heart, take it seriously, repent and make a decision to rid your heart of the malady. If you do not, you leave God no other choice but to humble you.

Spiritual Dreams Communicate Warnings

Warnings allow us to prepare or avoid the worst possible situation. When you purchase a product, generally it contains a warning label. The manufacturer of the product assumes no liability for the misuse of the product. The warning was provided to protect you, the user of the product, from harm or danger. If you use the product without regard to the warning, you can endanger yourself and in some cases, others depending on the type of product. The manufacturer isn't personally acquainted with you or other consumers of the product. Their goal is to sell as much product as possible and free themselves of incuring any additional expenses associated with the consumer's use of the product. Unlike the manufacturer, God is highly concerned about every detail of our lives and he uses dreams to communicate warnings. We must be open to receive and take seriously dreams that provide warnings.

I had a warning dream concerning the safety and protection of my sister. At the time, my sister was living alone in a new suburban community. In my dream, I saw thieves approaching her rear door trying to break-in. As I began praying, the thieves ran away. I awakened with a deep sense of urgency to pray for my sister, her safety and the protection of her home. I committed to earnestly pray for my sister. Approximately, two weeks following the dream, I received a phone call from my sister. She advised that there was a rash of home burglaries in her community. Electronics, valuables, and treasured items of residents had been taken. My sister told me that burglars attempted to break-in to her home through the rear door but was unsuccessful. When the law enforcement officials visited her home to get the details for the filing of a police report, they commented that she was blessed to not have been a victim. The burglars were entering through the rear door of the residents homes. I then relayed the details of my dream to her and she rejoiced. She began thanking God for his protection. I believe if God had not given me the warning dream and pressed on my heart an urgency to pray, my sister's home may not have been spared.

There were dreams noted in scripture after the birth of Jesus that provided warnings. These warnings were given to protect the life of God's only begotten Son. After the birth of Jesus, the wise men were warned of God in a dream to not return to Herod. Herod had plans of finding the young child Jesus and killing him (see Matthew 2:12). Prior to settling in a place to call home, Joseph and his family went to the land of Israel but Joseph did not want to live there after hearing that Herod's son was ruling in place of his father. After being warned of God in a dream, Joseph took the young child Jesus and his mother Mary to the district of Galilee to live in a town called Nazareth (see Matthew 2: 21-23). God's plan was to preserve his Son for the purpose of humanity's redemption. Now, we can experience the power of redemption because God's plan prevailed.

Spiritual Dreams Communicate Heaven's Initiatives

Spiritual dreams can be used as a way to communicate your involvement in releasing an initative from heaven. The Apostle Paul was informed by way of a dream that he should journey to the region of Macedonia to preach the gospel to its residents (see Acts 16:9, 10). This is commonly referred to as the Macedonian Call. While sleeping, Paul had a vision of a man beckoning for him to come to Macedonia to preach. Paul, not having traveled to Macedonia previously, took this dream literally and understood it to be a heavenly assignment. Paul, along with a few companions went to Macedonia and ministered the gospel of Jesus Christ. While in Macedonia, Paul and his companions encountered a woman with a demonic spirit who followed them around declaring in a loud voice that they were servants of the Lord. This woman was a fortune teller whose demonic gifting brought much gain to her owners. Paul became annoyed with the activity of this demonic spirit and after a few days, he cast the demonic spirit out, freeing the woman from its influence. The owners were furious and had Paul and Silas thrown into jail with the intent of bringing some type of criminal charges against them. Paul and Silas were not discouraged as a result of being jailed. Both offered prayer and praise to the Lord that caught the attention of those jailed and the prison guards. Their rendering of prayer and praise prompted heaven's intervention. The foundation of the prison was shaken, all the doors were opened and everyone's chains were loosed. It was evident that their visit to Macedonia was worthwhile. Their visit resulted in several people being saved, including the family of the prison guard and people witnessing the supernatural power of Jesus Christ. When God releases an initiative from heaven, the lives impacted are far more broad reaching than we ever anticipate. Our responsibility is to allow his divine plan to unfold.

Heavenly Dreams

We will spend all of eternity in our heavenly dwelling. Therefore, it is important throughout our walk of faith that we have experiences, dreams and visions of this grand place called heaven. I don't think God purposed for us to only become familiar with heaven when we depart this physical life, but we should see and experience it while we are here on earth. We should be interacting and experiencing the joy of heaven as it is the place of our eternal citizenship. Heaven is not a distant land that we are only priveleged to experience once we physically depart. But, it is to be experienced throughout the journey of the believer.

Throughout my life of faith, I've had dreams of heaven. Heaven is grand and its endless beauty indescribable. The colors are rich and lively. Everyone is filled with joy, happiness and peace. After all, its heaven, the perfect dwelling place. Heaven is awesome! As a believer, you can experience the awesomeness of heaven and share its beauty with others.

Dreams have been a constant in my life since early childhood. I can remember as early as four years of age having dreams. As a child, I wanted my parents to take me to an amusement park. I was fascinated with the rides, candy, and animated characters. I'm sure living in a state known for numerous amusement parks for children and families to enjoy, sparked and heightened my desire. Each time I slept in a certain place of my home, perhaps this place was a portal, I would dream of an angel visiting me. This angel was dressed as a modern day man and quite cordial. I did not consider him a stranger. As a child, I knew he was an angel of the Lord and not a messenger of the enemy. I knew I was safe and that he would take good care of me. In each experience, this angel took me to an amusement park for my enjoyment. It was exciting to watch the rides turn in motion and see the lights. I remember having a great deal of fun. The following day, I awakened with a deep sense of satisfaction knowing that one of my desires had been fulfilled.

The Significance of Spiritual Visions

It can be risky discussing visions due to the subjectivity involved but visions should be discussed as they've played a significant role in God revealing his plans in the earth. Old and New Testament scripture reveal visions occuring in the lives of prophets, servants, kings, and common people. Visions are not indicators of one's level of spirituality. Visions or information relayed in visions should always be judged according to the word of God and align with scripture. If information relayed in a vision does not align with the word of God, you know it is not from the Lord and should be discarded.

Visions inspired by God or spiritual visions transcend the physical world and propels a heightened awareness of the supernatural realm. Unlike dreams which only occur while one is sleeping, visions are appearances that can be seen while one is awake. Visions can play a signficant role in the accomplishment of your divine purpose and should not be taken lightly. Visions can help to formulate and shape our understanding of spiritual truths and kingdom of God principles. The Apostle Peter's trancelike vision revealed that salvation was not limited to the Jewish community. But, salvation was for the Gentiles who were once estranged from the covenant promises of Israel. The Apostle John had several visions while banished to the island of Patmos. John provided a written record of his visions in the book of Revelation. God desires that we know his future plans so that we can play an active role in bringing his plans to earth.

Spiritual Visions Provide Instruction

In Acts 10: 1- 7, we read about a centurion named Cornelius, who had a vision while praying. In a vision, Cornelius was instructed by an angel of the Lord to send men to Joppa to find and bring to his home Simon Peter (i.e. the Apostle Peter). Cornelius was a devoted and honorable proselyte. He diligently followed the law of Moses and developed a consistent life of prayer. He was a generous giver who shared with those in need. Cornelius' family shared in his testimony as they were also devoted proselytes. God rewarded Cornelius for his sincere dedication to prayer and giving to those in need by selecting him to be a part of the opening audience of the salvation message to the Gentile nation. Little did Cornelius know at the time of the vision and angelic visitation that God would allow his acts of righteousness to serve as a blessing to the entire Gentile nation. Glory to God! The righteous deeds we perform are not forgotten by the Lord. The Lord will remember deeds motivated by a heart of love and reward us accordingly. It was through the ministry of the Apostle Peter that Cornelius and his household including family and friends were brought to faith in Christ. This would be the start of the Gentile nation coming to faith in Christ Jesus. God in his divine wisdom used the devotion and faithfulness of Cornelius, a centurion, to serve as blessing to the non-Jewish world. If you are a Gentile believer, you can thank God for the spiritual vision given to Cornelius and him following through on the instructions provided.

Spiritual Visions Provide Insight into Future World Events

Spiritual visions provide knowledge of world events and serve as a source of encouragement amidst life-threatening circumstances. I recall reading the account of believers who were assembled in prayer on behalf an African nation. The leader of the prayer group sensed a deep urgency to pray for the wicked government leadership and the state of affairs within that nation. While the group was praying, one of the participants saw a vision. In the vision, agents of the kingdom of darkness were approaching in the direction of their nation. However, while the group was praying the agents turned around and began moving in the opposite direction. The person revealed this vision and the leader of the prayer group encouraged the people to continue praying. As the believers continued to pray, it was revealed to the leader of the prayer group that only the power of prayer could bring victory over the plans of their enemies.   The believers were encouraged to continue serving God in spite of the government opposition and praying for the manifestation of God's will.   More than three years later, a revolutionary movement began in neighboring countries.   However, their country was spared and the military overtake planned by their enemies failed.   A wise leader who embraced the spread of Christianity was elected to power and the people were permitted to worship God in freedom.   This powerful breakthrough within that African nation and its government occurred as a result of the God given vision which revealed the plan of their enemies in advance and the believer's need to pray.

Shortly after the turn of the century, I saw a vision of conflict and war in the nations of Iraq and Afghanistan.   I was alarmed at the time, because there was no attention in the media about these two regions.   I sensed a deep burden to pray and intercede for our nation.   Approximately a year and a half following the vision, our nation launched a war on terrorism and engaged in war with both nations.   I thank God for the vision as I was able to pray in advance for our nation.   God will reveal future events by way of visions.   Be watchful for how God speaks to you concerning future world events and be ready to be prayerful.   In some cases, you may be able to stop the plan of the enemy.

Spiritual Visions and a Cloud of Witnesses

It is within the will of God that we have spiritual visions that allow us to receive blessings from those who labored for the kingdom of God in past generations.   We, along with those of past generations are partakers of heavenly blessings. Hebrews 12:1 says, *"Wherefore seeing we also are compassed about with so great a cloud of witnesses..."* The cloud of witnesses are those who fulfilled their divine purpose and completed their journey of faith on earth. These are the great heroes and heroines of faith who willingly took risks, sacrificed their lives, endured ridicule and scorn and denied themselves the pleasures of this world to pursue God's greater purpose for their lives. Hebrews 11 gives the account of some of these biblical characters. And, there are countless more whose names are written in heaven and have profoundly impacted past, present and future generations. Past servants who pioneered or advanced movements in the body of Christ that radically changed history. They have transitioned from earth to heaven and are most interested in us completing our journey of faith and fulfilling our divine purpose. God may give you dreams and visions that sometimes include servants of the past to provide comfort and encouragement as you move forward in your journey. In some instances, God may impart words of wisdom through these servants by the way of dreams and visions. In each vision or dream I've had of past servants of the Lord, I've learned to carefully note it in a journal, title it, and refer back to the journal entry at various seasons in my walk of faith. Noting your experiences is helpful and should be a common practice. If you've had a vision of a past servant and wondered what to do, remain abased and recognize that it is not of your own merit that you've had such an experience. When you maintain a humble stance, you demonstrate the ability to handle the experience and become a prime candidate for more experiences.

Key Principles

1. Dreams are common to the human experience.

2. We must sharpen our understanding of spiritual dreams from God so that we can accurately interpret the message(s) God is communicating.

3. Mysteries and keys related to the fulfillment of our divine purpose are unveiled through spiritual dreams and visions.

4. God reveals his future plans to us through spiritual visions.

Prayer

Lord, speak to me through spiritual dreams and visions. Let supernatural experiences be a part of my journey to fulfill my divine purpose, in Jesus' name, Amen.

Study Questions for Chapter Seven are on pages 161 - 162

Conclusion

Hear counsel, and receive instruction, that thou mayest be wise in thy latter end.

Proverbs 19:20

Time Management

Our ability to effectively manage time will determine the assignments and tasks we accomplish related to the fulfillment of our divine purpose. If we spend time on futile efforts, we have less time to spend on worthwhile and kingdom of God building efforts. Jesus' parable of the wise and foolish virgins is a lesson that teaches the importance of obedience. Obedience has been emphasized throughout the lives of various biblical characters examined in this book. When you examine the parable of the wise and foolish virgins closely, you see that the importance of effective time management is also being emphasized. In the parable, there were ten virgins (see Matthew 25:1–13). Jesus makes a distinction between the ten virgins noting that five were wise and the remaining five were foolish. All ten virgins had lamps and were required to keep these lamps filled with oil so that they were ready to meet the bridegroom. They were awaiting the arrival of the bridegroom, whose unannounced appearance would be at any time.

The five wise virgins were skilled at effectively managing their time. This is demonstrated in their actions as they got sufficient oil for their lamps in advance of the bridegroom coming. They were prepared and ready for the bridegroom's arrival. The wise virgins are representative of those who make the most of their time. When you make a conscious decision to maximize the time you have been given, you tend to focus on the accomplishment of tasks related to your divine purpose. You are least likely to spend your time being idle and unproductive. On the other hand, those who do not recognize the importance of maximizing their time, waste the time they've been allotted. They are dependent on others just as in the parable; the foolish virgins were dependent on the wise virgins to provide them with the oil needed for their lamps. The foolish virgins failed to take responsibility for ensuring that they were prepared and ready to meet the bridegroom at his arrival. Time must be valued and held in high regard if you want to complete your journey of faith and fulfill your divine purpose. I learned that you must establish boundaries when it comes to scheduling and managing your time. If you do not establish boundaries, you are vulnerable to others establishing boundaries for you. Boundaries established by others are hard if not impossible to maintain and can lead to frustration. Do not overcommit. Recognize that you cannot accomplish it all. Look at delegating certain tasks and responsibilities to others with the expertise or willingness to complete tasks. Delegating tasks may require that you train or coach the individual but this is to you and the other person's advantage. They are learning and you are becoming skilled at communicating responsibilities.

My career has helped me to develop a useful technique for effective time management. I've learned to greatly appreciate assignments that require extensive research and delving into various legal requirements. This appreciation was developed over time after completing compliance reports, responding to numerous inquiries from elected officials and managing staff. I establish a timeframe to complete the most important and time sensitive tasks first followed by the least important task. An assignment that does not have a deadline date is given attention and taken care of within a reasonable timeframe. If I have to respond to a business inquiry, I give sufficient time to respond. This alleviates the notion of crowding my day and placing unrealistic demands on my time. Sometimes it may be best to set aside an assignment for a brief period of time. You may have to handle a pressing issue. I've had to so the same. This is acceptable. However, when you decide to place an assignment aside because of an unwillingness to complete or failure to do the required work, this is problematic and it reinforces lethargy. There are various tools and resources available online and in textbooks about effective time management techniques. You are encouraged to research these for your understanding.

Stress Management

Managing stress plays a key role in us fulfilling our divine purpose. If we are unsuccessful at managing stress, it will be difficult for us to fulfill our divine purpose. Stress can be brought on by our own desire to take on or do too much. We may want to quickly bring the plan of God into manifestation instead of patiently waiting for the plan of God to manifest in our lives. We see from the lives of Sarah and Abraham that impatience will cause for us to make unwise decisions. Commit to be in God's will for the appointed season of your life. It is stressful to live against the will of God. It will bring a weariness to the mind. *"Many are the plans in a man's heart, but it is the Lord's purpose that prevails"* (Proverbs 19:21, NIV). Allow God's purpose to prevail and be satisfied.

We are inundated with strains on our time and resources. We are presented with the challenge of combating stress daily. As a manager, I sometimes have the tendency of taking on the stress of meeting tight productivity goals that are placed on my staff. I care much for my staff and want to ensure that I am supplying them with the tools and resources necessary to effectively do their jobs and accomplish the mission of the company. If you are in a managerial or leadership position, you can unconsciously take on the burden of your subordinates, if you are not careful. I find that allocating time in complete isolation to meditate on the Word of God is helpful when I am challenged with stress. It clears my mind from the cares of the day and allows me to focus on God. Also, I wrote a simple prayer that I use when I encounter a stressful situation. If you are challenged with managing stress, you may incorporate the prayer below into your prayer time.

> Lord, I submit my susceptibility to stress
> to you. Your strength is made perfect in my
> weakness. I ask for your grace to be at work in
> my life, giving me power to triumph over this
> obstacle. I declare that I am an overcomer.
> Thank you for granting my request in Jesus'
> name, Amen.

When I encounter a complex situation, I've incorporated the following steps in my life to help with mitigating the vulnerability to stress. One, I focus my mind on the greatness of God. I acknowledge that no matter how challenging the circumstance appears, it is not greater than God. Two, I remember that my heart's desire is to please God and my actions must demonstrate this heart's desire. I make an effort to carefully monitor how I communicate. I don't want to pass any negative thoughts, feelings or emotions to anyone. This is not good for me or anyone else. I remind myself of the need to be optimistic. Three, I listen to soft, peaceful music that allows my mind to be at rest. Our world is filled with noise generated from car horns, the sound of automobiles traveling at high speeds on highways, televisions, cell phones with multiple ringing options, the sound of various computer applications, and the list continues. We are flooded with various sounds and just plain noise. It is good to clear our mind of all the noise so that we are in a state of rest. Good decision making derives from a clear and focused mind. I've lived in a big city filled with noise and a township of peace and serenity. My preference is living in a place of peace and serenity. It allows me to forget about the noise polluted world that I encounter when I commute to the big city for work daily.

Partnerships with Seasoned Believers

Prayerfully consider the need to formulate partnerships with seasoned believers. Seasoned believers are those who demonstrate spiritual and life maturity. They do not have a reputation of constantly being at odds with others. They demonstrate the love of God and desire to see Christ perfectly formed in the people of God. Partnerships should be formulated with seasoned believers who are focused on helping others in the body of Christ mature in the Christian faith. The purpose of partnerships is to provide you with a means for accountability and allow you to disclose your experiences in a transparent manner. Accountability obligates you to account for action items requiring follow-up, plans you've developed or commitments you've made to your partners. Partners should provide you with encouragement, counsel, guidance and support as you pursue and fulfill your divine purpose. This can be a team of believers or one believer. If you are a female, you should formulate partnerships with seasoned women of the faith. If you are a male, you should formulate partnerships with seasoned men of the faith. I do not encourage opposite sex partnerships. These are a NO! Partners should be objective in their approach and discussions with you. They should be committed to pray and intercede for you. As a matter of fact, I highly recommend an intercessor as one of your partners. I've found partnerships with seasoned believers to be very beneficial. I receive counsel and support. They are committed to pray and intercede for me. When I call, usually they are available. If they are not available, they will return my call within a reasonable time. As with any action plan, I encourage that you discuss this with your pastor or ministry leadership for confirmation.

Rely on God's Grace

Grace is God's endowment of supernatural power to accomplish that which is virtually impossible when attempted in human strength. We are totally dependent on God's grace to accomplish his purposes. Without grace we are left powerless and unable to successfully accomplish the will of God. The Apostle Paul stressed his reliance on God's grace. *"But by the grace of God I am what I am: and his grace which was bestowed upon me was not in vain; but I labored more abundantly than they all: yet not I, but the grace of God which was with me"* (I Corinthians 15:10). It was not by accident that Paul (formerly named Saul), one of the primary antagonists of the New Testament church would emerge to be one of the greatest proponents of the gospel of Jesus Christ. Paul said, *"For I am the least of the apostles, that am not meet to be called an apostle, because I persecuted the church of God"* (I Corinthians 15:9). Prior to his travel to Damascus, Saul was busy threatening the church and endorsing the persecution of many Christians for their unwavering faith in Christ. The purpose of Saul's travel to Damascus was to seize and arrest Christians who were preaching and teaching in the name of Jesus Christ. He had received authority in the form of letters by high-ranking religious leaders to search homes and gathering places to apprehend Christians. But, an unplanned encounter with Jesus significantly changed Saul's life. While on the road to Damascus, Jesus appeared to Saul asking a thought provoking question, *"Saul, Saul, why persecuteth thou me? …. I am Jesus whom thou persecutest: it is hard for thee to kick against the pricks"* (Acts 9:4,5). Saul was presented with this major life question. Would he continue persecuting the One he encountered? Would he continue to break the heart of His creator and consent to the torture of His followers? Saul's initial response was "Lord, Lord, who art thou." After Jesus revealed who he was, Saul inquired of what assignment the Lord would give him to undertake. Thank God, Saul surrendered to Jesus. Although there were others traveling with Saul, scripture notes that they were speechless as they heard a voice but did not see a person. Saul's encounter with Jesus significantly changed, for the better, the remainder of his life story. Paul learned that an immeasurable amount of God's grace was extended to him. Paul said, *"And I thank Christ Jesus our Lord, who hath enabled me, for that he counted me faithful, putting me into the ministry; Who was before a blasphemer, and a persecutor, and injurious: but I obtained mercy, because I did it ignorantly in unbelief. And the grace of our Lord was exceeding abundant with faith and love which is in Christ Jesus"* (I Timothy 1: 12 – 14). Paul acknowledged that without the grace of God he would not have accomplished the tasks and ministry assignments he was given that helped to advance the gospel message. Paul wrote several encouraging letters to his mentees and local churches which became known as epistles, completed several missionary journeys spreading the gospel, and maintained a committed life of prayer and study. The former could have only been accomplished by the grace of God.

Grace infuses us with the ability to operate, perform and achieve beyond human limitations. We learned from the experiences of the patriarchs Sarah and Abraham, Joseph, and Job that God does not reveal all of the details or particulars involved in our journey to fulfill our divine purpose. Understanding the totality of our divine purpose is a lifelong pursuit. As we consistently walk by faith, we begin to see the unfolding and fulfillment of our divine purpose. Our commitment to rely on and live by the grace of God will lead to the completion of a successful journey. When we receive his grace, we just as the Apostle Paul give the Lord permission to do a mighty work in our lives.

Key Principles

1. Effective time management is invaluable and places us in a state of readiness to accomplish the plans and purposes of God.

2. Stress management is critical to fulfilling your divine purpose.

3. Formulating partnerships with seasoned believers provides accountability.

4. Decisions that please the heart of God have a profound and lasting impact on our lives and lead to the fulfillment of our divine purpose.

5. Understanding the totality of our divine purpose is a lifelong pursuit.

6. God's grace gives us the supernatural power to perform and achieve beyond human limitations.

7. When we rely on God's grace, we give God the opportunity to do a mighty work in our lives.

Prayer

Heavenly Father, I receive your grace to wisely and skillfully manage daily affairs. Your word tells me to not have any anxiety or stress. Therefore, I give all of my concerns and cares to you. Help me to identify the seasoned believers you have equipped to serve as a source of support and encouragement in my life. I rely on your grace to fulfill my divine purpose, in Jesus' name, Amen.

Study Questions for the Conclusion are on pages 163 - 164

Appendix One

Instructions for Study Questions

Study Questions can be completed in individual or group sessions. Study questions are designed to reinforce important lessons learned and spiritual truths revealed in each chapter. Questions also include assignments to support continued spiritual growth and encourage you to take steps toward the accomplishment of your divine purpose.

Individual Sessions

Individual sessions are with you and the Lord. You can do individual sessions at any time. I highly recommend completing the study questions for each chapter shortly after reading the chapter. This will allow for the information and lessons learned to be fresh in your mind. Based on your individual spiritual needs, you determine how much time should be spent on each set of study questions.

Group Sessions

There are a total of eight sessions, one session per chapter. When conducting group sessions, listed below is a recommended outline to follow. The prayer included in Appendix Three can be used for the Prayer of Salvation. The prayer at the end of each chapter may be used as the Concluding Prayer.

Introduction and Opening Prayer
Chapter Review
Study Questions
Prayer of Salvation
Concluding Prayer

Group sessions are 40 – 60 minutes. Attendees are encouraged to be open and transparent about their experiences. Challenge yourself to invite a friend, colleague, and/or family member to a group session. (You may be surprised at the number of people who are seeking answers related to their divine purpose.) Show the love of Christ and during your personal prayer time; pray that the invitee will enter into a personal relationship with Jesus Christ. Group facilitators should be sensitive to the leading of the Holy Spirit and ensure that group sessions are tailored to meet the spiritual needs of the group.

Note

Before each session, think of ways to integrate spending quality time with the Lord. Allow the Holy Spirit to minister to your heart. Keep writing tools with you during this time so you can make note of what the Lord is revealing to you. Share your note with the group and discuss its relation to the fulfillment of your divine purpose.

Appendix Two

Study Questions

Chapter One
Destiny Altering Decisions

1. In the life of Sarah and Abraham, what sparked their initial destiny altering decision?

2. According to Genesis 12:5, what action did Sarah take after God gave the call to Abraham?

3. According to Genesis 12:7, what can be implied concerning the role Sarah would play in bringing to pass the promise God made to Abraham?

4. In your journey to fulfill your divine purpose, God will require that you make destiny altering decisions. Has God given you a divine directive that will require making a destiny altering decision? What is the directive?

5. What impact will obeying this divine directive have on your life?

6. Have you begun obeying this directive? If not, establish a timeframe to obey?

7. Are others involved in your destiny altering decision? If so, how will their lives be impacted by your obedience to this directive?

8. Has God revealed a promise that will accompany your obedience to his divine directive? If so, what is it?

9. Have you consulted with your Pastor or ministry leadership about your divine directive? If not, consider scheduling a time to receive counseling and guidance.

10. How will your destiny altering decision lead to or build on an established legacy of faith?

11. Complete a family tree tracing back to three generations. If you have enough information, you can trace back more than three generations. What traits do you see in your family tree? What is the legacy of your family? If your family legacy is an asset to future generations, what are you doing to continue this legacy? If a liability, what are you doing to bring about change?

Chapter Two
Character Development

1. Describe Saul's character before and at the start of his kingship.

2. Describe Saul's character during and at the end of his kingship.

3. What contributed to the demise of Saul's character?

4. What was the meaning of Joseph's two dreams?

5. Why was it important for Joseph to interpret the dreams of both prisoners?

6. Describe Joseph's character before and after his rise to prominence in the Egyptian kingdom?

7. Identify a challenge you've encountered in your journey of faith that could have led to the forfeiture of your divine purpose. How did you handle the challenge? What important lesson(s) did you learn?

8. Why is it important to develop character?

9. Think of a challenge you've experienced. What aspects of your character were revealed during the challenge? Were there shortcomings revealed that required attention? How did you address the shortcomings?

10. How was your character strengthened after you gave attention to the shortcomings revealed?

11. In hindsight, would you have acted or responded differently to the challenge experienced? Why or Why not?

Chapter Three
Carnal vs. Spiritual

1. Describe the war that exists between the carnal nature and the renewed nature in Christ?

2. How can we exercise control over the carnal nature?

3. What were the three prevailing issues at the Corinthian church during the time of Paul's writing?

4. How did Paul describe the Corinthian church in I Corinthians 3:3? Why?

5. According to Romans 8:7, what is the inherent nature of the carnal mind?

6. What is the nature of the spiritual mind? What are two benefits of being spiritually minded?

7. Define spiritual atrophy. Why is it important to avoid falling into a state of spiritual atrophy?

8. What steps can be taken to renew the mind? Why is it important to have a healthy thought life?

Chapter Four
Spiritual Warfare

1. What is spiritual warfare? What does spiritual warfare involve?

2. What is the purpose of spiritual warfare?

3. List the weapons of warfare. How can each of these weapons be used to defeat the kingdom of darkness?

4. What action(s) did King Jehoshaphat and the people of Judah take that led to victory over their enemies?

5. List the keys to victory and success during warfare. Discuss the keys to victory and success in detail. What is the importance of each key? What purpose does each key serve?

6. Think of time you utilized one or more of the keys to victory and success. What was the outcome?

7. What are the advantages of sharing your testimony of victory with others? Be willing to share your testimony with the group.

Chapter Five
Wilderness Seasons

1. How are wilderness seasons characterized?

2. What is the purpose of the wilderness season subsequent to salvation and early in our faith walk?

3. What advantage does wilderness seasons serve? Provide an example from scripture that details each advantage.

4. Describe the Old Testament character Job. What did Job learn during his wilderness season? What can you learn from Job's wilderness season?

5. Have you experienced a wilderness season? Describe what your wilderness season entailed. What did you do to navigate through your wilderness season? What lesson(s) did you learn as a result of experiencing a wilderness season? What advice would you give to someone who is undergoing a wilderness season?

6. Given what you now know about wilderness seasons, would you have acted or responded differently during your wilderness season?

Chapter Six
Prayer and Intimacy with the Lord

1. Define prayer. Why is prayer of great importance?

2. In St. Luke 18:1, what does Jesus say about prayer?

3. What are two commonly practiced prayers? Define each commonly practiced prayer.

4. What are the benefits of prayer? Have you experienced at least one benefit as a result of your prayer life? If so, please explain.

5. What are the hindrances to prayer?

6. What is the blessing that a consistent life of prayer brings?

7. What biblical character was identified as having lost focused and became sidetracked by a distraction? What was the distraction? What lesson can you learn from the life of this biblical character?

8. What is the "Resemblance Effect"? How is the process of resemblance described? What happens as we continue to make contact with heaven?

9. Have you experienced a distraction from intimacy with the Lord? When did you recognize that it was a distraction? What did you do to exercise authority over the distraction? What was the outcome? Share your testimony.

10. Take time to intercede on behalf of the needs of another person. Make a record or log your intercession in a journal. Believe God to intervene on the person's behalf. Remember to record how God intervened. Be willing to share with the group.

Chapter Seven
Spiritual Dreams and Visions

1. Define dreams. What three types of dreams are identified in Chapter Seven?

2. In Genesis Chapter 18, what Old Testament patriarch had a supernatural experience with the Lord through a dream? What type of supernatural experience did the patriarch have? What promise did God provide to the patriarch in a dream?

3. In Daniel Chapter 4, what Babylonian king had a dream that required interpretation? What was the condition of the king's heart at the time of the dream?

4. What role did the prophet Daniel play with helping the king understand his dream?

5. What was Daniel's reaction and response when he provided the king with the interpretation of his dream?

6. Describe some of the ways spiritual dreams can be used.

7. Has God communicated a message to you through a dream? If you were able to interpret the message, what was it? How has the message enhanced your life? How has it contributed to the fulfillment of your divine purpose? If the dream requires interpretation, consider scheduling a time with your Pastor or ministry leadership to discuss the dream. Be prayerful concerning the interpretation and its application in your life.

8. Define spiritual visions.

9. List three roles spiritual visions play. Why is it important to have spiritual visions?

Conclusion

1. Why is time and stress management of great importance? What can happen if time and stress are not properly managed

2. Discuss a challenge(s) you have experienced with effective time management and/or stress management. How did you handle the challenge? What important lesson did you learn while undergoing the time and/or stress management challenge? Develop a plan of action that will help you overcome the challenge(s) encountered.

3. Have you formulated partnerships with seasoned believers? If so, who initiated the partnership? In what way(s) has the partnership helped in your journey to fulfill your divine purpose?

4. What is grace? Describe how God's grace is at work in your life right now.

5. Discuss your journey to fulfill your divine purpose.

6. How has this book impacted the fulfillment of your divine purpose?

7. Share some of the experiences you've had while reading this book. How has your walk of faith been challenged?

8. Identify other keys that will assist you with fulfilling your divine purpose. Have you incorporated these keys into your daily practice? What steps are you taking to ensure these keys are being followed?

9. List one valuable lesson you've learned as a result of reading this book. How has the lesson learned impacted your perspective of your divine purpose? If you have not done so, make a commitment to the Lord to fulfill your divine purpose. Keep a journal of your journey.

Appendix Three

The Salvation Message

If you are reading this book and have not received Jesus Christ as Lord of your life, consider making the decision to accept Christ. God has great love for you. He loved you so dearly that he sent his only son Jesus into the world to die for your sins. Jesus suffered much pain and agony during his crucifixion on the cross of Calvary so that you may live free from the curse of sin. Seriously consider your need to accept Jesus Christ as Savior. He is the only Savior for you. When you make the decision to receive Christ, you are taking the first required step toward living a divine purposed life.

The Bible says, *"For God so loved the world, that he gave his only begotten Son, that whosoever believeth in him should not perish, but have everlasting life"* (John 3:16). You do not have to continue living with the conscious thought that when you die or physically depart this earth, you will not be ready to enter Heaven. You can have the assurance of eternal life in Jesus by accepting Him as your Lord through this simple prayer of faith:

Heavenly Father,

I acknowledge that I am in need of salvation. I repent of my wrong doing and right now I make the choice to receive your son Jesus as my Savior. I make the decision to turn from my old life of sin and rebellion against you and accept the abundant life of Jesus Christ. I believe that Jesus Christ died on the cross for my sins and that He rose on the third day for my right standing with you. I receive your gift of salvation in faith in Jesus' Name, Amen.

Praise God! You have received the Heavenly Father's gift of salvation.

Welcome to the Family of Jesus Christ!

About the Author

Mary Elizabeth Foster has been living a devoted life to Christ for nearly twenty years. She loves God and is dedicated to assisting the people of God advance to the next level of faith. She is a licensed evangelist and teacher in the body of Christ. She has ministered to incarcerated women for more than sixteen years witnessing many salvations, healings, and deliverances. She serves as team leader of the women's ministry at her local church.

Her academic success includes a Bachelor of Arts degree in Sociology from the University of California at Berkeley and a Masters of Social Work from the University of Michigan at Ann Arbor. While studying at the University of Michigan, Mary met her husband Benjamin. She has been married for the past eighteen years and is the mother of three children (Anna Danielle, Benjamin Micah and Eden Elizabeth). She considers it a great joy to care for and minister to the needs of her family.

Mary has nearly twenty years of experience in Human Resources Management. As purposed by God, the agency that gave her a start in the Human Resources field was looking for a candidate with a social work background.

Mary attributes all past, present and future success to God the giver of all blessings. She is a native of Northern California and resides in Southeastern Michigan with her family.

Contact Information

For additional copies of this book or to schedule Mary E. Foster for an event contact:

Mary E. Foster
E-mail: foster7610@gmail.com

God bless you.